FOUR TO THE POLE!

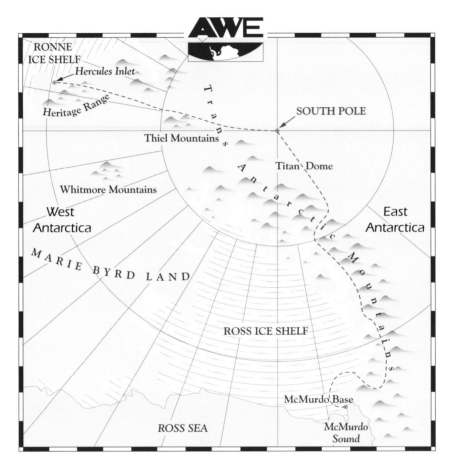

The proposed traverse of Antarctica by the American Women's Expedition is shown here in the broken line which runs from Hercules Inlet on the Ronne Ice Shelf to the South Pole, and from there to McMurdo Sound.

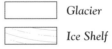

Glacier

Ice Shelf

FOUR TO THE POLE!

THE AMERICAN WOMEN'S EXPEDITION
TO ANTARCTICA
1992-93

by Nancy Loewen
and Ann Bancroft

Linnet Books
North Haven, Connecticut

Text © 2001 Nancy Loewen and Ann Bancroft.
Photographs © 2001 yourexpedition.com
All rights reserved.
First published 2001 as a Linnet Book, an imprint of
The Shoe String Press, Inc.
2 Linsley Street, North Haven, Connecticut 06473.
www.shoestringpress.com

Library of Congress Cataloging-in-Publication Data

American Women's Expedition to Antarctica (1992-1993)
    Four to the Pole!: the American Women's Expedition to Antarctica,
    1992-93/ by Nancy Loewen and Ann Bancroft.
        p. cm.
    ISBN 0-208-02518-9 (lib. bdg. : alk. paper)
    1. American Women's Expedition to Antarctica (1992-1993)—Juvenile
literature. 2. Antarctica—Description and travel—Juvenile literature. 3. Women
adventurers—Antarctica—Juvenile literature. [1. American Women's Expedition
to Antarctica (1992-1993) 2. Antarctica—Description and travel. 3. Adventure
and adventurers. 4. Women—Biography.] I. Loewen, Nancy, 1964- II. Bancroft,
Ann. III. Title.
G850 1992 .A43 A44 2000
919.8904—dc21   00-034929

The paper in this publication meets the minimum requirements
of American National Standard for Information Science—Permanence of
Paper for Printed Library Materials, ANSI Z39.48—1984. ∞

Designed by Carol Sawyer of Rose Design
Printed in Hong Kong by C & C Offset Printing Co., Ltd.

To my daughter Helena:
May you, too, grow up to ski across continents.
—N.L.

To the supporters of AWE for their belief in the project
and for helping us make history by putting us on the icecap.
—A.B.

Contents

ACKNOWLEDGMENTS

Thanks to <u>yourexpedition.com</u> for generously donating the map and photographs used in this book. Thanks to those whose letters are quoted. Thanks to editor and publisher Diantha Thorpe. And thanks to Ann Bancroft, Sunniva Sorby, Sue Giller, and Anne Dal Vera for their willingness to share this story in such a personal way.

A Note on the Text

This is a book of voices. The journals of the team members of the American Women's Expedition (AWE) are the primary sources, supplemented by material from AWE newsletters, transcribed tapes made for AWE, letters from family members, and poems quoted by the team members. Transcripts from the University of Minnesota, made as part of a psychological research project, also appear here.

For the sake of clarity and focus, I sometimes deleted parts of the entries. I added explanatory notes and bracketed phrases, where necessary, and made some minor changes in regard to spelling and punctuation. In just a few places I altered the words slightly, to make the meaning more clear. Otherwise, the words from the journals and transcripts, as they appear here, are the women's own entirely. —N.L.

INTRODUCTION

Long ago, the ancient Greeks believed in the existence of a vast land that lay far south. It had to be there, they reasoned, to balance the land in the north. Because the earth's northernmost region was called *Arktos*, meaning "bear," the mystery land to the south was called *Anti-Arktos*, or "opposite *Arktos*." Eventually it would become known as Antarctica.

During the eighteenth and nineteenth centuries, explorers sailing ever further south proved this belief correct. In 1773, Captain James Cook of Britain became the first person to cross the Antarctic Circle. In 1820, Fabian Gottlieb von Bellingshausen of Russia became the first to see Antarctica. The following year, the American John Davis actually landed on the continent.

Many of the early explorers were sealers or whalers. They faced the world's coldest, stormiest seas in order to hunt the abundant seals and whales that lived off the coast of Antarctica. With every expedition that took place, more was learned about the mysterious land. There were no native people, no trees or shrubs, no land animals. The climate was bitterly cold and

AN ANTARCTIC PROFILE

Antarctica covers 5.4 million square miles, about one and a half times the size of the United States. Ice and snow are spread across 98 percent of the continent. On average, the ice is nearly two miles thick, and the entire ice cap is very, very slowly moving toward the sea.

Temperatures vary considerably according to season and location. During the Antarctic summer, the coastal areas regularly reach freezing point (0°C)*. At the South Pole, the temperature ranges from -20°C in summer to -70°C in winter. The lowest temperature ever recorded was -88°C, at Vostok, a Russian research station.

In Antarctica, precipitation is in the form of snow. Coastal areas might receive the annual water equivalent of 10 inches, while the interior of the continent receives only about 2 inches. Blizzards occur frequently, as do whiteouts, in which low clouds or blowing snow make it impossible to see the horizon.

A surprising number of life forms have adapted to the harsh conditions of Antarctica. Many species of algae, moss, lichen and fungi have been discovered. Tiny insects, such as midges and springtails, survive as well. In addition, the cold waters of the surrounding ocean are rich with krill, fish, squid, seals, and whales. Penguins occupy some coastal areas, as do petrels, cormorants, terns, and other seabirds.

Signs of past life lay buried deep in the ice. Fossils from trees, ferns, fish, and dolphins reveal that Antarctica was once much warmer than it is today. Scientists believe that the continent was once located near the equator. Over hundreds of millions of years, the land drifted to the bottom of the world.

---

*   Temperatures are given in the Celsius scale. To convert to the Fahrenheit scale more familiar to Americans, multiply a Celsius temperature by 9, divide by 5, and add 32. Therefore -20°C would equal -4°F.

windy. Ice cliffs up to 200 feet high lined parts of the coastline. Though nearly all of the land was covered in snow and ice, the continent received very little precipitation each year. Antarctica, as it turned out, was a desert—the driest, coldest, windiest place on earth.

During the early 1900s, several attempts were made to reach the South Pole, the very bottom of the earth. No one succeeded until December 14, 1911, when Roald Amundsen of Norway and his team triumphantly planted a Norwegian flag at the site. Using sled dogs, they had covered up to 25 miles a day, reaching their goal in fifty-seven days.

Just a month later, on January 18, 1912, a team led by the Englishman Robert Falcon Scott reached the South Pole after a difficult journey, only to find that Amundsen had been there first. All five men died on the return trip. When their bodies were found, Scott's diary was tucked under his arm.

Sir Ernest Shackleton, also of England, was another prominent Antarctic explorer. He is best remembered for a trip that never happened. In January 1915, his ship, *Endurance*, became trapped in the ice of the Weddell Sea. The ship drifted for months until the ice finally crushed it. The men abandoned ship, camping on ice floes for six months before the sea opened up enough for them to use their lifeboats. They went through one ordeal after another—including, for Shackleton, an 800-mile journey over frigid seas in an open boat—before being rescued in August 1916.

During the late 1920s and 1930s, the new technology of flight was utilized in the effort to learn more about Antarctica. Hubert Wilkins of Australia made the first flights over the continent. In 1929, Richard Byrd of the United States flew over the South Pole, and in 1935, Lincoln Ellsworth, another American, became the first to fly across the entire continent. Following World War II, the United States Navy made great progress in mapping the coast and interior; the operation employed twenty-three aircraft, thirteen ships, and 4,700 men.

The International Geophysical Year in 1957-58 was another landmark in Antarctic history. Scientists from sixty-seven countries worked together, studying topics that ranged from glaciers and climate to gravity and outer space. Twelve permanent bases were built, including the Amundsen-Scott base at the South Pole. Also in 1957-58, Sir Vivian Fuchs of England became the first person to cross the continent by land. He and his team traveled 2,158 miles, using dog teams and snow tractors.

In 1961 the Antarctic Treaty went into effect. The twelve nations signing the treaty agreed that the continent "shall continue forever to be used exclusively for peaceful purposes." Besides prohibiting military operations, the treaty bans nuclear testing and the disposal of radioactive waste. Many more nations have since signed the agreement.

Today about a thousand people, mostly scientists, live in Antarctica year-round. During the summer season, which lasts from November to February, up to four thousand more people live at the various bases. Among the issues being studied are ozone depletion of the atmosphere and global warming.

Although much of the mystery surrounding Antarctica has been lifted, modern explorers are still drawn to the ice-covered continent and the challenges it offers. Improved technology has made their trips less dangerous than in years past, but the risk of injury, illness, or death is still very real. Radios can fail. Wind and snow and rough terrain can keep rescue planes from landing. No amount of technology can change the fact that Antarctica is the most remote place on earth.

Some expeditions try to recreate famous trips from the past, while others focus on being the first to go a certain distance or try a particular route. In 1985-86, for example, Roger Swan, Roger Mean, and Gareth Wood retraced Scott's journey to the South Pole. In 1989-90, Will Steger and Jean-Louis Etienne led a six-man team across the widest part of the continent, covering 4,008 miles.

Most explorers, to the Antarctic and elsewhere, have been men. But that is changing. Women explorers have their own dreams to pursue. Like the men who undertake these adventures, they have the desire to test themselves—their bodies, minds, and spirits—to the utmost.

The American Women's Trans-Antarctic Expedition, known over time as the American Women's Expedition, or AWE, was one such group. In November 1992, this four-woman team began its own trek across Antarctica. It was a journey that would make history, and one that would have a great impact on their lives.

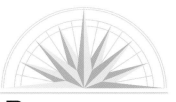

PROLOGUE

NOVEMBER 9, 1992

A small plane lands on a 50-foot patch of smooth snow. The door opens and is grabbed away by strong winds. Four women emerge from the plane. They begin unloading equipment—cross-country skis, sleds, tents, enough food to last for weeks. Their movements are slow, hampered by the wind and a temperature of -20°C, and by the layers of clothing they must wear in order to function in such conditions.

Finally all their gear is off the plane. One of the two pilots asks, half joking, if the women are sure they don't want a ride home. The women good-naturedly refuse the offer, though, and soon the plane is on its way, wagging its wings as a final farewell. Within moments the plane is gone.

The women are alone. Around them, stretching vast and white and wild, is the continent of Antarctica.

"Welcome home!" says the group's leader.

Ahead of these four women is a formidable goal: to cross Antarctica by ski, spending an estimated three and a half months on the ice and traveling 1,500 miles. There will be no snow tractors, no sled dogs, no outside assistance other than a few carefully planned food drops. Each woman will haul a supply sled weighing 200 pounds when fully loaded. If they succeed in making the traverse, they will be the first women to do so. If they succeed, they will also, along the way, become the first women to reach the South Pole on foot.

For now, though, there are more immediate concerns. At 46 miles per hour, the wind is too strong for skiing, so they must set up camp. They put up the two tents and build a snow wall to protect themselves from the worst of the wind. Unnerving mishaps occur: a gust of wind nearly carries away a sleeping bag, and does carry away a hat. The stoves don't work and have to be taken apart and tinkered with before the women can sit down to a much-needed hot drink and supper. The women speak very little, exchanging only those words needed to complete their various tasks. Hanging heavily over them is a fog of mixed feelings—excitement, worry, fatigue, and most of all a sense of respect for this great frozen continent that is beneath their feet at last.

The wind blows hard all night.

THE JOURNEY

"This expedition represents overcoming struggles to actualize dreams."

Ann Bancroft, expedition leader

Like many human endeavors, this historic Antarctic expedition started out as a vague longing that only gradually took on the weight of reality. It was Ann Bancroft who first conceived of the trip. A native of St. Paul, Minnesota, Ann had been fascinated by cold, faraway places ever since she was a child. She liked to read accounts of early explorers, and as a teenager and young adult she took part in many activities that developed her skills in the outdoors: camping in both summer and winter, backpacking, running, canoeing, skiing, mountain climbing, and sports of all kinds.

It wasn't just physical competence that Ann developed in those years. She came to understand a great deal about patience and persistence as she also struggled with dyslexia, a learning disability. Reading and math were difficult for her, because letters and numbers would appear to be mixed up. She also had a hard time retaining information, even about subjects that were important to her. But over time, she learned strategies for dealing with her disability. When she graduated from the University of Oregon with a degree in physical education, it was a special triumph for her. Other triumphs were in the wings.

For a number of years, Ann taught physical and special education in Minneapolis. Then her life took a different turn. In 1986, when she was thirty-one years old, Ann Bancroft became the first woman to travel across the ice to the North Pole. She did so as the only woman in the eight-member international expedition led by Will Steger and Paul Schurke. Using dogsleds and skis, the group traveled more than a thousand miles from Ellesmere Island to the North Pole. That success gave her the encouragement she needed to start thinking seriously about an idea that had long been in the back of her mind: to lead an all-women's expedition across Antarctica.

Planning for a major expedition is nearly as challenging as the expedition itself. So many aspects of the trip need to be considered, including the route, terrain, weather patterns, clothing, equipment, food and water supplies, transportation to and from the starting and ending points, and, finally, finding the right mix of people to accomplish the expedition's goals.

As Ann began to talk about her idea, her friends and family gave her their support, and soon others, too, became interested in the trip. A non-profit agency, the American Women's Trans-Antarctic Expedition, was set up in 1989 to handle fundraising and publicity for the trip. It would grow to include more than 150 volunteers and two paid full-time staff members. Ann Bancroft's private dream had become a public entity.

Four years passed as the expedition slowly took shape. This would not be merely an attempt to be the first in the record books, although certainly that was part of its appeal. AWE hoped to accomplish more than that. Its mission statement described these goals:

- To focus attention on the achievements of women

- To teach children about the continent of Antarctica

- To make people aware of the environmental issues facing Antarctica

- To assist in physical and psychological research related to women in extreme conditions

- To encourage people of all ages to take on new challenges

Teachers, schoolchildren, environmentalists, women's issues advocates—people of all ages and backgrounds found something to relate to in the expedition. Support for AWE came in the form of children's allowances, proceeds from school fairs, small checks from individuals, and donated clothing and equipment.

Unfortunately, support did not come in the form of corporate sponsorship. This is how expeditions are usually funded, because the costs are so high. Will Steger and Jean-Louis Etienne's six-man traverse of Antarctica in 1989-90, for example, cost $11 million. For most Antarctic expeditions, transportation to and from the continent is the biggest expense. Expeditions that aren't government-sponsored have only one flight company, Adventure Network International (ANI), available to them. Prices are high because of the risks involved, due to Antarctica's stormy weather patterns.

Ann scaled back her budget to under $1 million, but still found it difficult to raise enough money. The only corporations offering financial assistance were from the tobacco and beer industries, and AWE had to reject them because of its commitment to education and the environment.

Lack of sponsorship was a serious drawback. Ann was convinced that some businesses backed away from sponsoring the team because of fears that the women would fail—that they might need to be rescued, or might even die, which would create a negative image of the sponsoring company. Other businesses may have felt that there wouldn't be enough media attention to make sponsorship worthwhile.

The shortage of funds had an impact on the structure of the trip. Originally, the team was to travel a similar route to that taken by British explorer Sir Vivian Fuchs in 1957-58. His team traveled from the Weddell Sea to the Ross Sea on snow tractors—the first traverse of Antarctica. But about six months before the AWE expedition, Ann changed the starting point of the trip. The new starting point was Hercules Inlet, at the edge of the Ronne Ice Shelf. This point was chosen because it was closer to ANI's base camp, which meant that the cost of the flight would be reduced. It also took 200 miles off the distance of the trip. Still, the starting point was at the edge of the continent, which was important in order for the expedition to count as a traverse.

Although budget concerns were always present, the enthusiasm and the small but heartfelt donations of AWE's supporters buoyed the spirits and determination of the team. Even before the women set skis on the continent of Antarctica, they were making history as a grassroots expedition.

A team was assembled, but, due to injury or other conflicts, it would change several times before the actual journey. The four women who got out of that plane on November 9, 1992, were Ann Bancroft, Sue Giller, Anne Dal Vera, and Sunniva Sorby.

In her mid-forties, Sue Giller was the oldest member of the team. Her age was a concern, as she worried about having the physical stamina to keep up with the others. On the other hand, her many years of experience would be a great asset to the group. From Boulder, Colorado, Sue had over twenty years of mountain-climbing experience, and was also a longtime ski and climbing instructor. She had taken part in seven major Himalayan expeditions, as well as climbs on Mount Everest, Mount McKinley, and other major mountains.

From "Pulling Together,"
AWE's newsletter, winter 1991/92

Sue Giller is a detail person—the organizer, the planner, and one who is very likely to tell it like it is.

"Somebody once told me that my fatal flaw is that I'm too honest," said Sue, a computer programmer and longtime mountaineering instructor.

Among her cohorts, Sue is known as a solid veteran climber who shuns unnecessary risks but who also craves a good challenge. She remains a stickler for detail. She also remains ultimately team-oriented.

"All of us may have different expectations, but we're working toward something that's mutually rewarding," Sue said. "Our goal is not just to traverse the continent but to also work on team building."

Anne Dal Vera was a certified ski instructor from Fort Collins, Colorado. She also taught wilderness courses and led canoeing, rock-climbing, mountaineering, and even llama-packing trips for a women's outdoor adventure program called Woodswoman. In 1987, Anne completed a 600-mile canoe trip in Canada's Northwest Territories.

**From "Pulling Together,"
AWE's newsletter, spring 1992**

In the story of this ever-evolving adventure, Anne's part is very much in keeping with her character: one of tenacity and focus, integrity and follow-through.

Asked what she might discover in Antarctica, she believes it will be an exploration of the inner self. Then she laughs. "I don't know what I'll find, since I haven't found it yet!"

Anne's strength is in finding satisfaction in the day-to-day work of accomplishing a difficult, all-encompassing task.

"She has her eye on the goal but her hands in the moment," notes Rocco Dal Vera of his sister. Anne herself maintains, "What keeps me going is the enjoyment I have in doing what I do every day."

Sunniva Sorby, from San Diego, California, joined the team less than a month before the expedition. She replaced Sara Harrison, who had to pull out due to an injury.

It was risky to add a new team member so close to their departure, but also necessary if the trip was to take place at all. The team's equipment was set up for four, and their training was as a four-member group. To go with three people would have been dangerous, Ann Bancroft felt, because one would always be left out. She didn't want to postpone the trip, either. Delaying it for another year would have added a great deal to the financial and emotional cost of the trip, for everyone involved.

Ann's search for a new teammate ended when she met Sunniva Sorby. Sunniva had studied and worked in Norway and had traveled extensively in the mountains there. In San Diego, she managed the Adventure 16 Outdoor and Travel Outfitter stores and also taught navigation, rock-climbing, and backpacking courses.

From "Pulling Together,"
AWE's newsletter, winter 1992

She had heard about the American Women's Trans-Antarctic Expedition (AWE) some time ago, but thought her role would be to support it from afar. Little did Sunniva Sorby know that she would fly to Minnesota to meet team leader Ann Bancroft and teammate Anne Dal Vera, and a mere three weeks later be headed for Antarctica.

"It's hard to explain, but it really feels like this is where I'm supposed to be," the self-proclaimed 'eternal optimist' said.

Sunniva characterizes herself as a hard worker—one who has trouble accepting anything without effort.

"I was, from early on, taught that working hard was good for you," she said, "and that meant that everything I got I worked for."

As the newest member of a team that has been together for two years, Sunniva said it will be important for her to jump in and make her contributions. She's also sure that this trip will challenge her to grow.

"I thrive on challenge," she said. "I'm always wanting to take risks; I'm always wanting to push myself. This is really a big chance for me to walk my talk."

It was a competent team, with each member possessing the skills that the continent of Antarctica would demand of her. The women knew not to take chances. They knew that in such a remote location, even small mistakes could lead to devastating consequences. A minor injury, untended, could turn into a life-threatening condition; a tent not properly set up could blow away in a sudden gale. Their years of experience had taught them these lessons, and they felt they would be relatively safe in Antarctica. Yet, as most explorers do, they all made out wills before the expedition. And they discussed what their wishes would be if the worst happened and they died on the ice. Each woman chose to have her body placed in a crevasse* and left behind.

Nothing could be taken for granted. Even with their level of experience, the women needed to get to know each other and learn to work together. They needed to test their gear. They needed to develop strategies for everything from managing their food supplies to building the snow walls that would protect them from the wind. To that end, AWE went through two training trips. (Because she joined the team so late, Sunniva didn't take part in these trips.) The first one took place at Great Slave Lake in the Northwest Territories, Canada, in 1991. It lasted thirty-five days. The second one was a 300-mile, six-week trek across Greenland in the spring of 1992. During that trip the women dealt with malfunctioning stoves, strong winds, illness, frostbite, tendonitis, blisters, and a desperate need to push on and make miles in spite of the obstacles—all of which they would contend with in Antarctica.

---

*   A crevasse is a deep, narrow crack in ice or land caused by a split or cleavage. It is also called a crevice or a fissure.

Ann Bancroft, Sue Giller, Anne Dal Vera, and Sunniva Sorby.

But it was more than the physical aspects of the expedition that needed to be spelled out. For Ann Bancroft, the mistakes and successes of the training trips taught her the necessity of being a strong but flexible leader.

ANN BANCROFT
From an interview conducted by researchers
at the University of Minnesota

The leadership role doesn't mean that you have to snuff out people's voices and sort of think that you're the one to make all the decisions. But there is always a time in an outdoor trip where somebody has to gather the information and then say, "Okay, this is what we're going to do." But create an atmosphere where people can voice their opinions, however different they might be or difficult to listen to. So how do you create that environment and at the same time lay down the law when it needs laying down? And that's what I had to learn to do, just to stop that floundering and give our group a direction and a structure from which to work.

The logistics of the Antarctic expedition were finalized. On October 25, 1992, the team would depart from the Minneapolis-St. Paul International Airport for Punta Arenas, Chile. In Punta Arenas, the women would join up with ANI, the flight company that would take them to and from Antarctica. They would fly to Patriot Hills, ANI's base camp at the edge of the Ronne Ice Shelf. From there they would take a short flight to their starting point at Hercules Inlet. They hoped to be on the ice around November 1, the beginning of the Antarctic summer.

Their strategy was to start out slowly, making 8 to 10 miles per day, depending on the conditions. After they had adjusted to the physical demands of pulling the sleds, they would try to increase the miles to around 15 a day. They planned on reaching the South Pole by January 1, 1993, and then continuing the traverse. For this leg of the trip, they hoped to use a type of land sail; in the right kind of wind, the sails could boost their mileage considerably.

The team would arrive at McMurdo base on the Ross Ice Shelf no later than February 17, 1993. This last date was extremely important, for on that day an Australian cruise ship was scheduled to depart. If they couldn't make the ship, they would have to pay ANI to make a special trip to pick them up—adding $350,000 to the cost of the expedition. To an organization already seriously short on funds, this would be an enormous setback.

But it wasn't just the ship's schedule that determined AWE's timeline. It was the continent itself. The team would be traveling during the summer, with relatively mild temperatures and twenty-four hours of daylight. If the women remained much longer than the middle of February, the season would be over and they would face quickly deteriorating conditions—colder temperatures, increasing darkness, stronger winds, and unpredictable storms.

The plans were in motion. The team was prepared. It was time to go.

Leaving Minneapolis on October 25, 1992, was an emotional experience. Besides friends and family, dozens of AWE supporters came to the airport to see the team off. It was a powerful reminder that the four women who would be skiing across Antarctica weren't alone.

ANN BANCROFT
Journal entry

October 26, 1992

always take a deep breath going into the airport scene. It was calm at first. Some familiar faces, some not. A quick check-in as most everything was shipped. A bit of a heart throb thinking I might have forgotten my passport. So much to keep straight. Radio, video, BBC recorder*, my cameras, etc.

Suddenly I see cameras—a sea of AWE logos on white. Quick interviews, a few words of thanks and cheers. Strangers hugging you as if they know you. Wild. A last wave down the ramp and we are in the plane. The tears for me now cannot be stopped.

---

*   The British Broadcasting Company gave the group a special recorder for on-ice interviews.

Finally we pull away and I look out a slit in a window (we are tucked at the back of the plane) and I see again the sea of white T-shirts and sweatshirts waving. My eyes fill again and the people go from sight and I want more. Exhausted, but unable to sleep, I write thank-you letters. An endless stream.

Each team member knew that she would be faced with many, many challenges over the coming weeks and months. But the first major obstacle developed even before the team reached Antarctica. The women were stuck in Punta Arenas, Chile, much longer than expected. First, a mechanical problem delayed their flight, and they had to wait for a part to be flown in from Miami. Then poor weather conditions kept them from leaving. Since it would be a long flight, the weather patterns needed to be stable not just in Chile but in Antarctica too—and to hold long enough for the plane to return. Day after day passed by and the plane stayed on the ground.

The waiting took its toll. The women worried about how the lost days would affect them down the road. Financial concerns, too, weighed heavily on their minds, as AWE still hadn't raised enough money to pay ANI in full. They hoped that once the expedition got on the ice, the media coverage would generate more interest in the trip—and generate more cash as well. But for now, the plans and dreams of the past five years were at a standstill.

ANN BANCROFT
Punta Arenas, Chile

November 5, 1992

This is our eleventh day here. Again, our hope is that the weather system around Patriot Hills clears. This one around Punta stays good and we can make our eight-hour flight. We are about 50-60 miles behind our hopes. I keep telling myself it will be O.K.

17

As Gretel Ehrlich wrote in her poem . . . "I long for the ice to be my bed and the wind to brush my face, my bones."*

Still, the women did their best to keep their spirits up. It helped somewhat that they weren't the only ones waiting to leave. Several other expeditions— all men—were scheduled to take the same plane to the continent. Sir Ranulph (Ran) Fiennes and Mike Stroud were two British explorers who would be attempting a no-resupply** traverse. They were researching the effects of starvation on the human body and were raising money for the Multiple Sclerosis Society. Ehrling Kagge was a Norwegian who would be attempting a solo, no-resupply trip to the South Pole. There was also a Japanese research team that would be walking to the Thiel Mountains and on to the Pole, traveling a route that was similar to AWE's. The scientists would be taking snow samples, to be analyzed for evidence of atmospheric changes.

Everyone was eager to get on the ice and at least have a chance to do what they came for. But for the men, the financial stakes weren't quite as high. Their efforts were well funded by corporations or by their governments. If they needed to be rescued, they wouldn't be stuck with the tab.

At this point, Ann Bancroft still had a family member with her. Her sister Carrie had flown along with the team, and would be staying in Punta Arenas while the expedition took place. Her job was to monitor the team's radio contact and to relay information about their progress to AWE's headquarters in Minnesota. She would also be passing messages to the team and handling many other details as they came up.

---

*   These lines are paraphrased from *Arctic Heart: a poem cycle* by Gretel Ehrlich.

**   A resupply is a scheduled delivery of food, fuel, and any other necessary equipment. In expeditions without a resupply, team members must carry everything they will need for the entire trip. "Unsupported" is another way of describing this type of expedition.

CARRIE BANCROFT

from a letter to Carol North, expedition director

November 8, 1992

They're really something else, each one of them. I was very impressed with the way they handled the stress of not leaving from one hour to the next EACH day. I can't overstate their patience. Sue coped by sleeping and reading incessantly. Anne contemplated logistical questions. Sunniva was the one who ventured out and about and checked in on people's psyches by reading ancient Norwegian figures, playing and sharing her music or whatever. She was definitely the most hyper, physically. Ann became the comic and the clown and continually entertained us all. She was in particularly fine form in her interactions with the hotel staff, who grew to love us dearly.

Finally, at 12:40 p.m. on November 8, ANI was able to get a plane out. Twenty-five people boarded a DC-6 and set off on the long flight to ANI's base camp of Patriot Hills, Antarctica.

The women's first view of Antarctica was from a DC-6 approaching the Ronne Ice Shelf.

19

SUE GILLER

November 8 ▪ 4 p.m.

We are finally on the last leg before we start the pull. All of us and all of our gear flying in to Patriot Hills, due there in 4+ hours. This is a stage I never expected we would reach. At this point all bridges are burnt and we *must* go forward and *must* reach the Pole. At least it is now in our hands. After having felt so afraid of this trip for the past two weeks, I have finally made the crossover to acceptance of the challenge. I fear my body giving up and costing the others work—maybe even an evacuation if my ankle is bad. I don't fear the physical dangers or boredom or such, but the specter of failure mostly. The burden imposed by having all those people in the U.S. so connected to us is immense—I struggle under it.

SUNNIVA SORBY

November 8 ▪ 6 p.m.

We just passed the Alexander Islands. Outstanding! The ice beneath is oozing with a heavy mist and haze. It's another world down there. The ice is enormous. The hairline fractures [we see] from the air are something else to be reckoned with below. We'll be touching down on the last frontier in 2+ hours and I am so damn excited—I *must* keep breathing!!

That night at Patriot Hills the women checked their food supplies, which had been sitting in the belly of the plane for many days. They found that some of their cheese and meat had started to mold, so they replaced the spoiled food with additional butter. They also checked their other gear and filled their fuel bottles. Finally, around 5 a.m., they decided to sleep for a few hours in the Twin Otter, the plane that would be taking them to their starting point.

Organizing gear near the blue ice runway at Patriot Hills. The start of the expedition was now just one short flight away.

AWE WORKING EQUIPMENT LIST*

ITEM	WEIGHT IN POUNDS
4 sleds	4
4 pairs skis with poles and ski skins	
Upski land sails - chutes with harnesses and parts	20
4 daypacks, fanny packs, duffle bags, stuff sacks	
Weather gear	1
2 thermometers, 1 barometer, 1 anemometer	
Navigation, communications, and documenting gear	
GPS locator with solar panel/batteries	
compass with maps/photos	
watches	
ELT Beacon	
solar panel	
laptop computer	

*   Not all weights are established in this draft list.

Sony Hi-8 video camera
Nikkon FM-2 camera
film and batteries

Climbing gear

2 shovels	3
2 saws	1
1 55 cm ice axe	2
1 55 cm ice hammer	2
1 8 x 150 lead rope	10
ice screws (@ .3)	1
1 pulley	2
1 jumar set	2
full crampon and instep crampon	2
beaners	1

Camp supplies and food

2 2-person Kelty wind-foil tents with extra poles, tie-outs, etc.	7
tent stakes	4
4 sleeping bags with bivie, thermarest pads, thermarest foam	20
2 Optimus 1-11B stoves, one complete, one in parts	5
platform, insulation, and plastic funnel for stoves	1
fuel (30 gallons at 6 gallons each)	180
4 qt. insulated cook pot	3
4 qt. pot	1
2 frying pans with cooking spoon and spatula	1.5
4 thermoses, mugs, bowls, spoons	2
8 Nalgene fuel containers - one liter each	1
18 toilet paper rolls	7
food (2.5 lbs. per person per day to resupply)	393
first aid kit	8-10

Personal gear and clothing (for each member)

boots - one pair with overboots	1
down booties	0.5
wool socks - heavy/liner socks	0.75
underwear	0.5
Polypro bottoms and tops	2
pile bottoms and tops - one heavy, one light	
down jacket and pants	
wind jacket and pants	
gloves - contact gloves, heavy gloves, heavy mitts	
Polypro hood	0.25
wool hat	0.5
face mask	0.5
goggles - one pair	1
glacier glasses - one pair	0.5
toiletries	
miscellaneous: Nalgene water bottles, knife, lighter, pee bottle, books/journals and pens, research equipment	1

Repair kit

Leatherman, ski binding parts, sewing kits, stove parts, wire, duct tape, sled pieces, tools and screws, zipper heads, etc.

DAY 1

November 9

At about 12:30 p.m., the four members of the expedition were dropped off at Hercules Inlet, at the coordinates of 80°15′ S longitude, 77°06′ W latitude, their official starting position. They hooked up their sleds, organized their equipment, and distributed the loads so that each would be carrying about the same weight. It was too windy and the women were too tired to ski, so they decided that it would be safest to stay right where they were. By 4:00 p.m. they had built a snow wall and set up their tents. The first tent rotation was Sue Giller with Sunniva Sorby; Ann Bancroft with Anne Dal Vera. They planned on rotating tent partners every eight days throughout the journey, to help them develop unity as a group. The women cooked supper, crawled into their sleeping bags, and tried their best to sleep. Day 1 was over.

The expedition: each woman on skis, hauling a sled, sliding over Antarctica one step at a time.

*   Temperatures at start and finish, miles traveled, and position in latitude and longitude were recorded daily.

DAY 2
November 10

-15/-17°C, 4.8 miles, 80°19.35' S, 77°13.57' W

Anne Dal Vera

The wind blew hard most of the night. The snow wall blew down at about 6:30 a.m., but everything was fine. The wind died down about 9 a.m. We woke up at 7, got out of the tent at 10 and divided up the food. We are missing a bag of food. Bummer. Ten pounds I guess. It took awhile to adjust ski bindings, harnesses, and pack up. Clear sky a.m., cirrus clouds p.m. We skied for 5 hours 45 minutes, including two breaks. And we moved 4.8 miles. The sastrugi [hard ridges of snow] are very complex with holes everywhere. It is very hard snow, so the sleds glide O.K. We found a flat spot at 5:15 so we stopped. It took 2 hours to set up camp. The snow is hard.

Ann cooked *fantastic* beans and rice.

As the women expected, the physical demands of their new life on the ice took some getting used to. Sunniva developed two large, very painful lumps in her neck, a result of hauling the 200-pound sled. Sue developed tendonitis in her ankles. Ann developed frostbite on her thighs, and all three of them suffered from blisters on their heels. Only Anne Dal Vera got through the initial adjustment period without any serious complaints.

Although they struggled with pain and fatigue, they couldn't help but marvel at the secrets that Antarctica was revealing to them.

DAY 3
November 11

-21/-20°C, 5 miles, 80°23' S, 77°17' W

Sunniva Sorby

I am in constant awe about this continent. It is *so* vast and *so* beautiful. At about 9:30 p.m. the sun was starting to break, casting such a cold glow on the ice waves. The blowing snow moves over the hard pack and waves, in all directions. It's wild. While we're skiing I look around and at times I'll let out a scream. I cannot believe I am here.

DAY 7
November 15

Sue Giller

The terrain and sky are beautiful! Constantly changing light. Saw some glowing sun dogs* yesterday, caused by heavy ground drift. Double arc rainbows on either side and a wavy one on top of the sun. Very interesting and beautiful.

From the outset, one of the resolutions the women intended to honor was—to have fun. They wanted not only to stay friends throughout all the hardships they would face, but to become better friends. Though inevitably moods would change and there would be times when one or another would become irritable or pessimistic or detached, on the whole the women formed a very close-knit, cheerful group. They were there to put in the miles and make the traverse, but that didn't mean they couldn't enjoy themselves, too. So when Sue Giller turned forty-six on November 15, it was only fitting that they do a little celebrating.

---

*   Sun dogs, or mock suns, are luminous spots that appear on either side of the sun. They form when sunlight is refracted through ice crystals. *Parhelion* is the scientific name for this phenomenon.

Sue (left) and Sunniva during Sue's birthday celebration, complete with balloons in hats and libations in thermoses.

ANN BANCROFT

transcribed from a tape made for AWE

On the seventh day we celebrated Sue's birthday. I was tenting with Anne at the time, and we blew up balloons—it was pretty windy and we didn't know how to get them over to their tent so we put them in spare hats to carry them over there. We also put some goodies together, and then lit a couple of candles that were re-light candles—but even those had to be warmed up in order to get them to light and re-light again. We finally got them working, ran over to their tent, and barged in with balloons and the candles. Anne had made some gingerbread, well, they kind of looked like pancakes, but we called them cupcakes. We had a little swig of Sue's libation [Scotch whiskey], that she brings along with her, and brought her into another year.

On the eighth day, blowing snow prevented the group from traveling. It ended up being a rest day—and though the lost miles were a concern, everyone was glad for the chance to recover from the previous week's hard work: covering more than thirty miles with the sleds at their heaviest. The women caught up on sleep, wrote in their journals, did some sewing and tinkering with their gear, and let their blisters dry out.

DAY 8
November 16   -15°C, 0 miles, 80°41′ S, 77°27′ W

Sunniva Sorby

Today we were not able to venture outside. The snow has been blowing all night and all day today. It's now about 6 p.m. I haven't done much all day. Sue was up at 6 to make our first round of drinks. I didn't even touch my coffee I was so tired. Sue and Ann B. went back and forth about what we should do. When we should go. We decided to be on call for the weather to change. It hasn't changed all day. I can hear the snow crystals skate over the ice— sounds like something sizzling.

Fortunately, the next day the winds lessened and they were able to get back out on the ice.

DAY 9
November 17   -16°C, 8.4 miles, 80°56′ S, 77°34′ W

Sunniva Sorby

Today is my dad's birthday. I sang "Happy Birthday" to him on the trail. I thought of a lot of people today—it makes me really happy—makes me glide more.

By the time two weeks had passed, the women had settled into a fairly predictable routine. They woke up at 6:00 a.m., and in each tent the women took turns making breakfast. Then they put on their traveling clothes, packed their gear, and were out of the tents by 8:00. It took another 30-40 minutes to break camp and pack their sleds. They pulled for two to two and a half hours, took a fifteen-minute break (sometimes longer, if necessary) for a drink and something to eat, and repeated that routine all day long. Normally they skied single-file, switching leads after breaks to allow everyone the chance to break trail and set the pace. They stopped pulling between 6:30 and 8:00 p.m., unless injuries or fatigue caused someone to call for an earlier stop time. Around November 20 they decided to stop building snow walls around the tents unless the weather was threatening. That saved a lot of time and energy, and they were able to set up camp in about 20 minutes. The tentmates took turns cooking supper and getting water ready, so while one woman was taking care of those chores, the other had the opportunity to mend gear, write, tend to injuries, or just relax. That was also a time for them to talk to each other, since they couldn't talk much during the day. Then came bedtime, usually between 10:00 and 11:00.

DAY 14
November 22 -18/-11°C, 10.6 miles, 81°30' S, 77°44' W

Anne Dal Vera

Sunniva told me at a break, "This is day 14. Do you know what that means?" I said no. She said, "I've given myself two weeks to break in." So I said, "You're all broke in then. Congratulations," and we shook hands. She really did seem to be feeling better. She didn't look so stiff when skiing and she kept a good pace all day. No stops to stretch that I could see.

DAY 14
November 22

Sunniva Sorby

It was so silent all night. It's almost eerie when you don't hear the wind because it's usually always present. The sun was shining briefly as we stepped into the day. By about 1 p.m. all the clouds had moved past us and the sun was pouring down.

My heels are very ripped up with blisters. My hair is a greasy mess. My nails are growing and are cracking so I had to cut them (now that's a first, aye?). My lips are very sore from the wind and breathing. My eyes are always red and sore and puffy. My knees ache a bit and my whole body is a bit sore.

⁓⁓⁓

Day by day the women increased their mileage. In the beginning, when their sleds were the heaviest and the sastrugi more difficult, they made around 5 miles a day. Then they managed 6 miles a day, then 8, and then 10. They knew that soon they would need to do better than that, but they were making definite progress.

Though daytime temperatures averaged -15° to -17°C and there were usually winds from the south, the physical exertion of skiing and pulling sleds kept them warm. And in the tents, the twenty-four-hour daylight created enough solar radiation to allow them to stretch out in long johns rather than in bulky clothes. Sometimes, in the tents, it was almost bright enough for sunglasses.

DAY 14
November 22

Ann Bancroft
transcribed from a tape made for AWE

Today was a rare day when the wind died out. We have moments of that and we get pretty parched by the sun, and of course take off all of

29

our wind clothes and try and ventilate. When we are sledding we are so hot that the wind is actually a pain because we can't generally stay cool enough. Our torsos get so hot because they're in harnesses and the work is just so hard that you're working up quite a sweat. And you are trying very hard not to overheat because that gives you quite a chill when you stop. When we stop we get into down jackets so it's really quite a contrast. One minute we can be in shirtsleeves practically and the next minute we're in big bulky down jackets—and we're more than ready to go after the 15 minutes—in terms of our temperature, not in terms of our enthusiasm level—we're exhausted by all of this. We're actually climbing a great deal. Not just this first piece to the Thiel Mountains, but also all the way to the Pole. It's truly an uphill slant—one that's visual. I liken the ice to big swells on the ocean, where we go up and we go down a little bit, then we've got to go back up again.

Throughout the expedition, each woman went through her own highs and lows at different times. For Sue, the roughest part was in the beginning, the first three weeks or so. She struggled with fatigue and bad ankles. She worried about how long it was taking to adjust, and questioned her ability to stay with it to the end. But when one woman was weak, another was strong—and so the group forged ahead, hour by hour, striving to find a balance between the needs of all the members.

DAY 16
November 24   *no temperature recorded, 0 miles, 81°30' S, 77°44' W*

Sue Giller

After seven days of push, we have finally taken a rest day. The weather has been most cooperative—clear, warm (-15°/-20°C), mostly calm. The past three days we have made 25.5 miles,

Much of Antarctica's surface is covered with hard waves of ice and snow called *sastrugi*. The *sastrugi* patterns varied from one area to the next, and were often formidable obstacles for skiers dragging heavy sleds.

going each day until 6. We have decided not to build snow walls at every camp unless weather is threatening. That saves 30 minutes and lots of energy. As of 3 days ago, we needed to average 15 miles/day to make the South Pole by January 1. Anne Dal Vera still thinks we can do it. I haven't asked Ann Bancroft.

I still find myself wishing I wasn't here. I don't mind the tent life, or the weather—just the physical effort of daily pulling. I have been thinking of the office back in Minnesota and all the people who have worked to put us here, though, and that motivates me to continue and to try and improve my attitude.

31

DAY 17
November 25   *-12/-10°C, 11.8 miles, 81°47' S, 77°56' W*

Anne Dal Vera

We pulled 11.8 miles! Calm, clear, beautiful day. I led for a while at 2-3 p.m. I got a great rhythm and stride going and was thoroughly enjoying being out there, route-finding through a complex sastrugi pattern. Sunniva was dropping behind but I didn't notice. Ann caught up and said, "I know it feels good to stretch out, but please stay aware of the distance [between you and the others]. It can get very discouraging." I said I was sorry and pulled out at a much slower pace. I felt quite ashamed.

The team experienced several holidays on the ice, but their celebrations had to stay small-scale. For Thanksgiving, Anne Dal Vera cooked a dinner of turkey, vegetables, soup, potatoes, cranberries, and basil biscuits. Otherwise it was an ordinary pulling day. Mostly holidays were a time to think of people back home, wonder how everyone was doing, write letters, and maybe cry a little as a way to relieve loneliness and stress.

DAY 18
November 26: Thanksgiving Day   *-17°C, 10.9 miles, 81°57' S, 78°04' W*

Ann Bancroft

Skiing along these last few days, the ice has looked very much like the Serengeti Plains. White of course, but today I half expected the migration to begin. Wildebeests* moving in the distance. It's so vast and the treeless quality must give it that similarity.

---

*   When Ann was a child, her family spent two years in Kenya, Africa. Wildebeests are migrating antelopes with long, curving horns and tufted tails.

As we climbed at one point today, it was as if we were working our way to the end of the earth. At times you really get that "bottom of the world" feeling.

I brought out the Nutella [chocolate hazelnut spread] for Thanksgiving dessert. All in all a good day. Not much time for anything extra. Many thoughts traveled home today.

Besides keeping up with the daily chores of tent life, each member of the group had specific responsibilities as well. Sue was the navigator. She was the one who kept track of their position, making sure that as the women maneuvered around sastrugi and crevasses they didn't stray too far off course. They used a navigational device called GPS (Global Positioning System), a computerized box that received data from satellites in space. With this device they learned their precise location, mileage, elevation gain, and what bearing to take to get on course. The system used batteries, so every night in the tent Sue had to put a battery pack in her pants, warming it up enough to allow her to get the readings.

Anne Dal Vera was in charge of planning and organizing all the food for the traverse—about a thousand pounds' worth. Food was a critically important aspect of each day, both physically and psychologically. Each woman needed around five thousand calories a day to keep up with the demands of life on the ice—nearly three times what most women need in normal circumstances. Meals were high in fat, and included lots of cheese, butter, and meats such as bacon and sausage. Other basics included oatmeal, hash browns, rice, beans, and pasta. Between the staple ingredients and different spices and seasonings, the women were able to create a large variety of meals. In order to conserve fuel, the meals were usually cooked in one pot.

The women also needed to eat during their breaks. Since food freezes rock-hard in the cold temperatures of Antarctica, the women kept trail foods (such as cheese, chocolate, nuts, and dried fruit) in inner pockets of their clothing, using body heat to keep it at a reasonable temperature. They also kept thermoses of water or other drinks handy. Working as hard as they did, staying hydrated was a constant challenge.

Sunniva was in charge of the group's medical kit. This included medicines such as ibuprofen, eye salve, anti-diarrhea medication, and topical analgesic ointment; it also included first-aid items such as splints, gauze bandages, needles, sutures, tweezers, and iodine. She made sure the medical kit was well-stocked and kept track of what was being used.

Sunniva was also responsible for the research the group had agreed to do. Every three weeks, for a one-week stretch, the women took spit samples every three hours. After the journey, these would be evaluated by the St. Paul-Ramsey Medical Center in Minnesota. The researchers were examining changes in cholesterol and hormonal levels, immune system functioning, and the effects of living in constant daylight. In addition, the women filled out psychological surveys as part of a University of Minnesota study on extreme stress. These surveys explored issues of personality characteristics, group dynamics, and individual coping mechanisms.

While the women were committed to these research projects, the actual tasks could be annoying. In the dry air of Antarctica, it was sometimes difficult to muster enough spit for a sample. And the surveys, done in the evenings, required concentration at a time when the women usually just wanted to sleep.

Ann Bancroft was in charge of the radio. Every three days, in the evenings, she called in to the base camp at Patriot Hills. A radio operator there relayed the group's messages to Carrie Bancroft in Punta Arenas, Chile. Carrie then passed the information along to AWE's headquarters in Minnesota. It took a lot of time and it was often a frustrating task, since neither Ann nor Carrie could be sure that the other was receiving the messages correctly.

Ann Bancroft on the radio to Patriot Hills. This connection was the expedition's lifeline to the world beyond the ice.

ANN BANCROFT
from a tape made for AWE

We're using the dipole* on the radio, so we're having to set out a big T. A cord goes out from the radio inside the tent and that's sort of the bar of the T and then the cross piece would be two orange pieces of wire that have to be equidistant from each other. I'm hoping to put it in the right direction of Patriot Hills so that we can clearly hear them and they can hear us. It's a little bit of a pain to set up every three days, but it goes pretty smoothly—so far. If you can't get them on one frequency then somebody has to run out and roll it up to the next frequency and then you switch channels and try again.

---

*   A dipole is an antenna that is split at the center for connection to a
transmission line.

CARRIE BANCROFT
from a letter to Carol North, expedition director

November 30, 1992

Dear Carol,

Today I received a recording of the last radio contact with the team from the 26th, most of which I already relayed to you. Following is a transcript—Ann B. on radio with Max at Patriot Hills. The tape is in the mail:

Alpha Whiskey Echo, Alpha Whiskey Echo,* it's Patriot, good evening, you're loud and clear. How on us?

Good to hear your voice . . .

Good evening, it's Max speaking. You've just faded a bit. How do you copy me, over?

Sorry Max, copy really well, really well, over.

O.K. a little better that time. How are things, over?

Things are going really well. The weather is perfect, the weather is perfect. Things are going great. Over.

O.K. What sort of snow conditions are you in at the moment?

The snow conditions are hard-packed, a little bit of ice, no powder, no powder. Over.

Check that. What's your present position?

Present position: 81 57 decimal 1 south. 81 57 decimal 1 south. Over.

Charlie, Charlie.**

78 04 decimal 8 west. 78 04 decimal 8 west. Over.

O.K. Copy all.

We have sunny and clear weather, mornings are about 17 below. Over.

O.K. I check that. How many miles have you been doing on average? Over.

---

*   In radio communications, people often spell out words using a phonetic alphabet, in which each letter of the alphabet has an assigned word. "Alpha Whiskey Echo" stands for AWE.

**   In radio communications, "Charlie" means that the information has been heard and understood.

Average miles about 10 or 11. Um, today, 10.9, 10.9. Over.
[Pause] O.K. I'm just a little bit slow, I'm writing it down. Um. How's your equipment performing, your skis and sleds, etc.? Over.
[. . . unclear . . .] all gear is good, all gear is good. Over.
Well that's good. What about how are your bodies standing up? No blisters or anything?
[. . . unclear . . .]
Uh, you're very weak, very weak. I lost you on that one. Could you say again please?
Minor frostbite, lots of blisters and sore muscles. Minor frostbite, lots of blisters and sore muscles. Over.
O.K. Well that's to be expected. Hope you're looking after the blisters and the frostbite. And as you get a bit further along I'm sure the muscles will adjust a bit too. Over.
[. . . unclear . . .]
Sorry I didn't get that. Could you say again please. Over.
[. . . unclear . . .] one, one eight miles. Over.
O.K. I check that. 118 miles total.

[At this point another Patriot Hills staffer, Morag (Mo) Howell, comes on the channel. They talk about the progress of the British expedition, and then Ann asks her if there are any messages from Carrie. Mo responds:]

Negative. But I'll try and speak to her tonight and tell her how you're going on. Have you any message for her? Go ahead.
Just want to wish her Happy Thanksgiving, Happy Thanksgiving. Not to worry, we're going slow but steady.
O.K. I'll give her that message and see if she can ship down a bottle of Jack Daniels [whiskey]. Go ahead.
[. . . unclear . . .]
I said, I'll get her to ship down some Jack Daniels. Go ahead.
[Laughter] Sounds good Mo, sounds good. Over.

Maintaining regular radio contact was very important, not only to reassure family and friends that the women were all right, but also to back AWE's commitment to the educational aspects of the trip. More than 250,000 schoolchildren in the United States and Canada followed the group's progress through e-mail and recorded telephone messages. Teachers used specially developed curricula about Antarctica, in areas such as science, math, geography, history, and reading. Each day, as the women pulled their sleds a little closer to the South Pole, kids from kindergarten to senior high were learning more about the earth's mysterious seventh continent.

FAN MAIL

Dear AWE Team,
My name is Bobby B. I am in fifth grade. I hope you can do it. I think you can. That's a long way away. It must be hard to pull your luggage in back of you. What if you had to stop? You would bump into it and it will trip you. We are studying about you in my class. Will you get a reward if you cross Antarctica? I love skiing too. It is really fun. I really hope you do it. I give you my best wishes. Well gotta go.

Sincerely,
Bobby B.
Allentown, NH

As the days passed, the women continued to up their mileage. With their sleds becoming lighter, they stretched beyond the 10-mile range and now began making 11, 12, and eventually 13 and 14 miles each day. They were grateful that the weather remained consistent.

Often the outside world seemed far away—as if the women were traveling on another planet, or in a place where time stood still. Having given up, for a time, their normal lives back home, they tried their best to live in the moment. And that meant dealing with the demands on body and spirit, relying on each other, and allowing themselves to be fascinated by this ice-covered continent that was anything but boring.

DAY 19
November 27
—15/-10°C, 12.1 miles, 82°07′ S, 78°07′ W

Sunniva Sorby

It was really tough today—and I'm sure it'll get even tougher. It's such a whiteout here—when the clouds hang around you can't see a thing. Visibility is slim to none and Slim left town. We were being tossed around everywhere—it was hard on the stomach and legs. While we were climbing I had my head down most of the time—it's easier to be depressed that way—just kidding. At one point when I lifted my head all I saw was Anne D. buckle to her knees and down for the count. She was leading and it was pretty impossible to tell up from down and flat from huge mountain—she went over a sastrugi and poof! Thank God I was at the back because I could not stop laughing. I was concerned about her, but when I saw her get up I laughed—hard! Later in the day Sue did the same thing only she really wiped out—she was all tangled in her sled rods— Ann B. was leading the home stretch our last 40 minutes—so as a joke (since she had turned around to check on us) we all plopped down—comic relief!!

DAY 22
November 30
-15°C, 14 miles, 82°42.4′ S, 78°24′ W

Anne Dal Vera

It is such a beautiful day. Ann says she sometimes feels like we are hiking and just over that ridge is going to be a beautiful view. Only it isn't a ridge and the view isn't different. Still her heart races with excitement just to be here doing this.

It's 11:13 p.m. Bright in the tent and warm enough to not wear a hat or gloves. I sit in my sleeping bag with a hot water bottle in my lap. The sun is low now, to the south. It was in the west at 7 when we made camp and will be east when we wake up. It circles us round and round, highest in the north at noon. It never sets.

DAY 22
November 30

Sunniva Sorby

The time goes by so quickly when you stop at 6:30 or 7 p.m. You have to put your down jacket on, set up tents, dig up snow for the storm flaps, cut snow blocks for water, get your personal/group stuff unpacked, reclip* your sled—tie it to a stake, start the stove, make hot drinks, take off your boots (one of my favorites) and layers, sweep the kitchen area—and there's more. Lots of chores! It's now 10 p.m. and I can feel my hip, knees and quads throb. Time to take some aspirin.

I wonder how I keep going sometimes. Today I felt so depressed, like I could not go on. I needed to be held or to lay down and sleep—anywhere! At that point I was pretty desperate. What's terrible is at times I feel so alone in my hardships—like no one else is struggling—no one else has a heavy sled. This of course is not true—they simply have practice and experience at dealing with the pain and agony. I remind myself tonight that I do not need to be as good as or better than these gals—I need to find what works for me and stay with that.

---

*   To rebuckle the cover that went over the top of the packed sled.

Anne Dal Vera

I woke up at 2 a.m. and began to write the numbers I was thinking about. I was trying to come up with a formula for making it to the Pole by January 1 so we can do the whole traverse. Ann woke up and asked me what I was doing. I told her, "Number crunching. I'll show you in the morning." She said she had been doing that thinking too. So we got to talking and stayed up till 3:45. Ann wonders if we built too slowly at first. But Sue's feet were hurting some days and Sunniva's neck had bad pain and lumps.

We talked about Sue's belief in numbers and resulting pessimism. Sue will also at some point become extremely positive and ready to give it her all. She'll go the extra mile on less food when she sees there is a chance and it is necessary to push hard. But now she is saving herself because she believes she doesn't recover as quickly.

Sunniva has many symptoms now. Puffy eyes, chest cough with green-yellow phlegm, blisters and general malaise or tiredness. We puzzle about how to motivate her. She has more in her than she has given, but she's been plagued with pain.

Ann relies on me to help her stay positive and be steady. That feels good. We have a lot of potential as a group. Now we just have to reach it.

6:30 comes too early. I slept in! I hurriedly cook breakfast. Ann reassures me that it will be O.K. and refuses to get caught up in my rush.

We leave camp at 8:45 and I am the last one out. It is a beautiful day. Ann leads at a strong pace. Sunniva asks me, "Is Ann stressed about leaving camp late?" I say she's just committed to 14 miles today.

After 45 minutes Sue stops to pee and I pass her. She hollers at me that I will want to tighten the straps on my sled when I stop next.

I look back and my pack* is gone! I must not have strapped it on securely. We yell at Ann to stop. I get ready to ski back for my pack and Ann says, "Check the sled first!" We do, but I know it's not inside. As I take off, Ann cautions me, "Don't burn out now, just go steady." It is good advice.

It feels good to ski without a sled. Twenty-five minutes back to the pack, which made it a ways out of camp. Twenty-five minutes back to where I left the group. They seemed like small dots on the distant hillside. And as the clouds came across the sun I prayed the weather would not sock in while we were separated. It was a bit difficult to see the sled tracks in the hard snow and if we lost visibility I would have been in a dangerous situation. But it remained partly cloudy.

When I got to the group they had gone about a mile pulling my sled in tandem with Sue's. I told everyone I was very sorry to have made such a mistake and that I would be glad to do something to make it all up to them but I wasn't going to berate myself about it. Sunni said, "There is one thing you can do—that is to put it all behind you."

We skied 12.6 miles. It cost us a mile to go back for the pack. I was extremely tired when we got to camp.

Although the entire team was concerned with making more miles, it was Ann Bancroft, as the group's leader, who worried the most. If they were to have any hope of safely making the full traverse, they needed to pick up the pace—now. They needed to make miles in the mid to high teens, not the low teens. And in the short term, Ann wanted them to reach the Thiel Mountains as soon as possible. They would be receiving a food resupply in that area, and she hoped they could have a day of rest and then charge on.

But did they have it in them to push that hard? Ann was especially concerned about Sunniva, who had a respiratory infection. Though she was

---

* Each woman kept a daypack, which included a thermos, goggles, cameras, etc., strapped to the top of her sled.

taking medication for it, the long days of skiing were making it difficult for her to recover quickly. Still, there wasn't much choice. They had to keep moving forward.

On December 5, as she skied on steep, icy slopes against the wind, Ann worked out the agenda for a team meeting the next day. She felt it was time to try some new strategies.

DAY 27
December 5   -8°C, 12.6 miles, 83°33.8' S, 78°58.7' W

Ann Bancroft

Meeting tomorrow:

Sunniva—10 pounds given up. Get better—keep pace.

Everyone watchdog breaks—not just me.

Each 5 minutes we're late in the a.m.—add on. Solid 2 1/2 hour march. Pace stays steady until last 2 hours—or we just go longer.

Take care of each other. If that means cooking twice in a row then do it.

No day off unless weather or illness.

DAY 28
December 6   -16°C, 14.9 miles, 83°46' S, 79°08' W

Anne Dal Vera

Ann had everyone gather in our tent at 7:45 a.m. for a meeting. She mapped out her vision of what was to come and asked us to be committed to it and to the whole traverse. It was a direct approach. She was a bit nervous, I think—kept capping her pen, and her hands were shaking. I think it also reflects the depth of her desire and her need to have us all be invested in making the dream a reality. I like this style of leadership.

45

DAY 28
December 6

Sunniva Sorby

Our meeting this morning was a reality check for all of us as well as a time to refocus and gear up for a haul. I really plugged away today. I am really committed to making the traverse—I really want this for all of us—we can all taste it. Ann suggested that some weight be taken out of my sled to keep me from grinding down when I'm already ground. I am doing all that I can to get better and stronger. It's hard to feel too proud of yourself for making it through the day or pushing yourself harder than you've done because you know it's going to happen over and over again. I did feel proud today though—I kept a good pace and followed and stayed focused on every step. I had to—it took a lot of work given that I'm still struggling with my breathing and my energy. We have 6 more days to push hard and I'll do it—only one day at a time. I've been saying a lot of little prayers and inviting new thoughts into my mind—ones of encouragement, hope, and spirit. It helps to surrender yourself when you don't know what direction to take—inevitably it gives you that deeper breath you needed or better stride. There's hope for me yet.

After Ann's talk, the group was able to achieve a few high-mileage days. But then new obstacles developed that threatened their progress. Sunniva sprained her ankle, and Anne Dal Vera developed tendonitis. Ann Bancroft, who was still feeling strong despite frostbite and a badly bruised heel, remained frustrated in her role as leader. Like the others, she had to deal with the mixed emotions that the group's difficult venture brought out in her.

Ann Bancroft

feel as if I say the same things over and over. Stay on top of taking care. Sleep is key. I don't feel listened to and when folks get pooped and don't like the pace or can't keep it or talk about less weight I bristle. I feel as if I am working overtime to keep track of them, motivate them and even do/carry more than them. I keep trying to work on my expectations and attitude about this and I am faced with it again the next day. It takes away a bit from the progress we are making (for me). I struggle a bit to stay "up"—but generally this place wins out. It's beautiful and I love it. My childhood dream unfolding. I try and grasp that. This feels more profound than anything I've done. More amazing. I've wanted to do this for so long. Put together the project—lead it—do it.

As the women neared the Thiel Mountains, they began looking for a reasonably smooth place for the resupply plane to land. When they found one, on the evening of December 10, Ann set up the radio and called in to Patriot Hills. Then she had to check in with the pilot every hour or so to give updates on weather conditions. The plane arrived around 3:45 a.m. On board were two pilots, and a doctor who examined the women's various injuries and recommended courses of treatment.

The women received some additional gear and enough food and fuel to get them to the Pole. In exchange, they sent out letters, film, audio and videotapes, used batteries, the spit samples and psychological surveys, and any equipment they felt they wouldn't be needing. They also sent out their garbage. Recyclable items would be flown to Chile. Though this approach cost them in both money and extra weight, it was in keeping with the expedition's goal of respecting and preserving the environment.

In the shelter of the plane, everyone visited and relaxed. The women were treated to hot drinks, homemade pineapple cake, oranges, white chocolate, and cheese. Finally, at 8 a.m., the plane left, and the women went to bed.

DAY 33
December 11

Anne Dal Vera

We went outside to wave at the plane when it arrived. They circled us and flew back and forth across the sunny sky, taking several shots of us and the camp. All our gear was neatly lined up outside. It was very exciting. The landing was a direct approach from the north. The Twin Otter seemed to hover powerfully as it came toward us, then set down about 70 feet away and taxied to a stop with the wing right over our radio antenna. We cheered as Warren, Clay, and Tom all hopped out to shake our hands and congratulate us on getting here. The folks at Patriot Hills are very impressed with our progress and are all rooting for us.

DAY 33
December 11

Sue Giller

Resupply. Two days early (or rather, 30+ miles early). Plane came this a.m.—Twin Otter—and left our stuff. Thirty-two days of food, less fuel. We have 370 miles to the Pole. Everyone is upbeat and ready for the next go. I feel relatively recovered and hope the strength in my legs is there. I have definitely lost weight. I figure it will take us every bit of 32 days to reach the Pole—Ann Bancroft still hopes for less to have time for the traverse.

Considering the handicaps of the past month we have done well, and we need to push deeper for the next leg. I am motivated to reach the Pole—no wishful thinking when the plane left.

* * *

Though it was a great relief to have the first part of the trip behind them, the resupply meant that the women's sleds were heavy once again. For Sunniva and Anne, who were struggling with injured ankles, the extra weight was an especially difficult burden. Just three days after resupply, the group took another rest day, hoping that the time off would help heal injuries and boost energy levels for the hard push ahead.

Following the resupply, Anne Dal Vera began going through an especially difficult time. Prior to that point, she had experienced relatively few discomforts and had been optimistic about not only reaching the Pole but also completing the traverse. Now, however, the pain in her ankles and the relentless daily routine made her vulnerable to depression.

DAY 36
December 14

-16/-4°C, 0 miles, 84°50′ S,80°30.2′ W

Anne Dal Vera

Yesterday was hard for me emotionally. The sameness of the activity is wearing on me, giving me a weariness that is frightening. I even thought of suicide a couple of times. Of course I know that it would be easy to accomplish. And it would be absolutely devastating to so many people. That was enough to turn my mind away from the idea. Ann commented that I was very quiet and remarked on how the sameness of the activity was probably getting to me. I said, "Yes, that certainly is part of it."

DAY 39
December 17   \quad -16/-12°C, 11.6 miles, 85°18.6' S, 81°23.5' W

Anne Dal Vera

What an emotional day! I spent the first two hours of travel crying in my beak [face mask] feeling very sorry for myself. I fantasized about pulling up to the others at the break, plopping down on my sled and sobbing. Someone would come up and console me. I decided that would be a good idea, to reveal my emotions to the others. I really had to struggle with it though. My nature is to hide when

Sue Giller, Anne Dal Vera, and Sunniva on break. Something always needed to be done, so although the breaks were very welcome, they were not always restful.

I feel bad and try to pretend I'm O.K. It seems too embarrassing to put that out for others to see. I had a voice inside me saying, "Is this really necessary? Perhaps we could go on without creating a scene." But I knew I needed it. So after I put on my down coat, I moved the tent over and lay down on the sled. Ann asked, "What's wrong Anne?" I didn't respond. She asked, "Dal Vera, are you O.K.?" I shook my head and said, "I guess I just need to cry." And I did.

Sue said that when she was having a hard time early in the trip she would think of the sparkles in the snow as symbolizing all the people who cared about her. Ann reiterated that this is a difficult juncture in the trip, emotionally. As we skied off, Sunniva told me this quote from her Runes [old Norse poems] that helped her as a mantra when her neck hurt so bad:

> *You whose power illuminates the sun*
> *That shines over the whole world,*
> *Illuminate my heart*
> *That I may rise and shine.*

Anne later attributed the experience, at least in part, to the heavy doses of ibuprofen she'd been taking. She noted that, according to homeopathic* theory, mental and emotional states are more important than physical ones. Though the ibuprofen masked her physical pain, that pain was pushed to a deeper level and resurfaced as despair.

Slowly Anne's ankles improved and she began to feel more like herself. But she would have a hard time regaining her former energy and drive.

Sunniva, too, was wearing down under the strain of traveling day after day, mile after mile, in pain. One of her worst days came on December 24, Christmas Eve.

---

*   Homeopathy is the practice of treating illness with very diluted medicines that are based on natural ingredients.

Sunniva Sorby

I felt really desperate with how much I was hurting. I would pull aside and huddle between my ski poles—hang my head down and sob—for what seemed like a while. It was all I could do to keep the steps going. At about 10 a.m. Ann B. had stopped and waited for me. We talked for about 15 minutes about the realities of pain, spirit, and how to deal with it. She was pretty intense. She is constantly trying to juggle the outcomes of our days versus her reality. It's tough for her. She needed me to be very honest about the pain—is it getting worse, deteriorating with the push, or was my spirit low, down because I was hurting? She said it's important to separate the pain and the spirit. When we're low, feeling down, tired, dreary, pissy, grumpy, crampy, etc. we must move with that—feelings that do pass through. When we have an injury we really have to be careful. We have a lot of work to do down the road. I need to last and I need to get stronger. Ann hugged me for a while. I think she too had tears in her eyes. She said, "I need you on this trip. I need you to go to the Pole and I need you to go on to McMurdo. I knew I needed you from the day I met you." It hit me hard. I realize the strengthening effect I've had on the team. Despite my woes, pains, and setbacks I've been—I think—a strong contributor.

Ann said she knows there is something she is to gain from all this—I agreed too—but neither one of us can quite figure it out yet. Perhaps one day we will, perhaps we should just let it all pass and trust that we are on the right path and that each day may indeed be more difficult than the next. Oddly enough I'm somehow expecting that. As Dad would say, "Life wasn't meant to be easy."

On Christmas Day, the women slept in and settled back to enjoy a rest day. Everyone tried to be cheerful. Still, as they opened cards and small gifts from their loved ones at home, they all felt the stark contrast between past Christmases and this one, spent at the bottom of the earth.

That afternoon, Ann went for a long walk, talking into a tape recorder to the supporters of AWE. She knew that back in the United States, family and friends and supporters were hanging on every word that came from the team. They were keeping the team's story before the public, and were continuing to raise money through donations and loans.

As she spoke into the recorder, the empty white plains stretching out for miles all around her, Ann was reminded, again, that the women were far from alone.

ANN BANCROFT
From a tape made for AWE

I'm talking to you on Christmas Day, Christmas afternoon. We slept in this morning—an incredible luxury. I played Santa Claus last night; it was a lot of fun. We had a very difficult day yesterday because Sunniva's spirit died—we just weren't making much headway, we kept having to stop, shed a few tears. She's been on ibuprofen for so long for so many ailments that I think it is wreaking havoc on her system. So we took her off of it, and of course the aspirin wasn't enough of a pain reliever or an anti-inflammatory. It's hard to have an appetite when you're nauseous from all of that ibuprofen, and nuts and raisins don't really coat the stomach. So she had a tough day, and we knocked off at about 4:30 and only made about 7 miles—which actually was pretty good for the amount of time we shuffled. The conditions are also tough because we are going uphill, and we've got a little dusting of snow and it feels like someone is pulling the opposite way with your sled. So that's tough. The last several days have been very slow for the amount of work and pace that we feel like we're keeping—we're not getting the results we keep hoping for. Even though the sled weights are going down, I think it's more the mental thing, and I know certainly our bodies are tired. My knees ache and we all have flare-ups of tendonitis in various places in our legs. So we're all skiing with some discomfort. But by and large we're laughing a lot, we're getting along— very little tension for a group of four living elbow to elbow for 47 days. This is Anne and Sunniva's longest time out—maybe even Sue's, because climbing trips are so very different. So we've passed that mark of previous experience for most of the group, and we're entering into a new kind of time. My hope is that with the coming of the Pole there will be a new sort of energy, or a resurgence of energy—people will get ignited and be able to dig a little deeper into their emotional and physical beings and push out some more miles to make that date happen.

Back to Christmas. Last night we pulled in, and I really wanted the mood to be a positive one—especially after a day that was emotionally pretty difficult. I didn't find it to be physically as hard as many of our days, so I played Santa Claus. I stayed up until 11:30, tucked all of my little cherubs in bed, got out three of my clean socks and put little red cords on them. I made Sunniva a dreamcatcher out of Q-tips and dental floss. I made Anne a purple (the only color she seems to like—everything she owns is purple) triangle pile bag with all sorts of little warm fuzzies—little reminders of things that she likes. Of course, for Sue, what do you give Sue? Not something schmaltzy. No—you give Sue a pair of socks—dirty, sweaty, and used, but nonetheless socks. She is going through socks like nobody's business. She has different boots than the other three of us—and I don't know what the problem is—so she got socks from me. You know, nothing too schmaltzy. But I've been carrying around a lot of weight. I planned Christmas back in July. I brought a ton of powdered eggs (I know that sounds gross to you all), dried bell peppers (red and green), dried raspberries, and no-bake cookies (whatever those are). I left a portion at each door. I brought M & Ms, peanut and plain, and proceeded to stuff stockings with all sorts of little goodies from home. When everybody was sleeping, and I heard these little murmurs and sighs, and snoring, I proceeded to tiptoe out in my long johns to this other tent.

54

Expedition leader Ann Bancroft made Christmas happen by playing Santa—about as far away from the North Pole as a person can get!

There is actually a little chimney in these tents—sort of a little slit where the steam can come out as you're cooking. So I hung these two stockings in Anne and Sunniva's tent, and then left tons of food outside their door. I also left a note in their stockings that said, "Look out your door before you eat in the morning." I then hung a stocking for Sue as she snored away. Sue got pretty creative herself, actually, little bits of chocolate for me and a certificate for three hugs for Anne (that was a big one—the best gift ever). Sunniva had actually sent out her journal, thinking another one was coming in at the Thiels—but it didn't, so Sue gave her a bunch of paper, which is very valuable out here. So everybody did something in the way of Christmas cheer.

DAY 47
December 25: Christmas Day   *-16/-12°C, 0 miles, same position*

Sue Giller

Merry X-mas. It's been 10 long days [since the last rest day] of pulling and counting miles. Sunniva has had to deal with a lot of pain in her ankles, both pulling and at night when her ankles swell. Yesterday her spirit broke and Ann spent two different times talking to her—"either decide to call it [stop for the day], or push and deal with the pain." Slow snow with gentle climbing. Sunniva finally called it at 4:30 after a stressful day for all, worrying about her and our need to make miles (7.2 in about 5 hours). We are still on schedule for the Pole on the 10th. (12 miles a day would get us there on the 12th.) We will need to up the miles and the big question is Sunniva's feet and spirit. It's hard to tell what's wrong—tendonitis, I think. She apparently has bad ankles anyway. She has dealt well with it so far and will do well tomorrow. Anne is quite recovered spirit-wise and almost well foot-wise. She took some weight from me several days ago and that was a big help. I feel strong (but fatigue in the legs) and pointed to the Pole, but not beyond. I am getting quite thin. Today is a rest day and we are celebrating X-mas, trading little gifts and decorating the tents. It doesn't feel like X-mas with the 24-hour sunlight.

After Christmas Day, Sue Giller stopped keeping a journal. For her it was a coping strategy—she decided to put that time and energy into other areas of her daily life instead.

SUE GILLER
**From an interview conducted by researchers
at the University of Minnesota**

I started to keep a journal, but I was so tired that that was one of the things that was not important to maintain at the beginning. I got so far behind that I let it go and would only write occasionally, if something major happened. I vowed on this trip I would keep a journal, which I used to do, much more than I have in the last couple of trips, but I couldn't do it. Everybody else kept copious journals. I spent a lot of time journal-writing [in my mind] during the day. I mean that was one of the things I would occupy my mind with—letters and journal entries. And I found, at night, that I couldn't then sit down and repeat it. It was mostly internal dialogues, monologues, letter-writing stuff, what-ifs. I just didn't have the energy early on, and that was part of my survival mode: take that energy and sleep, take that time.

"The hard stretch has begun," Ann Bancroft wrote on December 26. She wanted the group to reach the Pole no later than January 10, rest there two days, then continue on. She was acutely aware that February 17—the date the cruise ship would leave from McMurdo—was quickly approaching. But between Sunniva's injured ankles, tougher conditions on the ice, and general weariness, it was difficult for the women to make the sort of miles they needed. They were actually doing quite well, averaging the right number of miles per day according to their original plan. The problem went back to those nine lost days in Punta Arenas. Somehow they needed to make up that time. Somehow they needed to stretch a little further.

DAY 49
December 27 *-14/-16°C, 12.9 miles, 86°50' S, 82°25.6' W*

Anne Dal Vera

The weather was overcast with low visibility. We crawled over some amazingly high sastrugi and bounced and jerked over smaller ones. I tried to videotape our progress in the poor light. Then I interviewed Ann at a break about what it felt like to find the way in that weather. She likes days like that so much.

The end of the day was so full of jerks and slides! Sometimes the sled would slide up behind me, then come to an abrupt halt, wrenching my gut. I called out a few times and tried all different adjustments to the harness. Oh!

Still, it was beautiful as the light slowly returned. It was still overcast, but gradually the ice began to take shape into the complex wind-scoured humps, knife edges, and fins we had been feeling under our skis. During the lowest visibility I had to tell myself, "Keep your head up and ski by feel."

DAY 50
December 28
-14°C, 11.5 miles, 87°00.4′ S, 82°37.9′ W

Anne Dal Vera

Ann led with a fast and hearty clip. We climbed a hill and she was off down the other side. Such a dramatic scene! Bright light down on the ice, then dark skies beyond and a disappearing dot that was Ann.

On the evening of December 31 (Day 53) the women celebrated the new year with Sue's Scotch whiskey and with some cinnamon schnapps and chocolate cherries a friend had sent along. But they couldn't stay up late, nor could they afford a rest day on January 1. Instead, they would be getting up at 5 a.m. in an attempt to get more miles out of the day.

As it turned out, the first day of the new year was not a day of hope or renewed determination. For Sunniva, it was perhaps the worst day of the trip.

Even in the best of circumstances, Sunniva and her team-mates faced immense challenges in their Antarctic journey. And when illness and injury struck, they had to tap into physical and emotional reserves they didn't know existed.

DAY 54
January 1, 1993
-17/-14°C, 12.6 miles, 87°46.6′ S, 83°23.7′ W

Sunniva Sorby

Today was my day of reckoning. I stumbled and fell amongst the company of my three teammates, the cold biting wind, the clouds and the white vastness of this wild, untamed desert. I certainly pick my places. I hit rock bottom emotionally and physically. I could not find the strength, will, nor reason to go on. I was, I thought, completely spent. For the last 53-odd days I've had some minor or major ailment to deal with and I've dealt with it. I never gave up, I kept going as strong as I could as hard as I could. In that process I was not letting anything or anyone in. From the first week I've been feeling really lonely and alone. Like no one knows what I'm going through or that what I'm going through is for me solely to deal with. A hard place to be in. I've been in constant turmoil about what to share with everyone. You know they care, you know they too have their own problems, you know you matter, you know you need to let others know but there's the proud, stubborn part that refuses to eek out an "I need help" or "I'm not doing so well." The reality of the matter is—out here—everything matters.

Too often I have needed to know the answers and needed to feel control. Being out here, in this unmistakably wild place, I feel no control. I feel only the seriousness of needing to take care of myself. I am learning how to do that to the deepest physical and psychological levels. My decisions have to come from me about me because this is all I really have out here. As I was releasing to Ann I told her about my feelings of having not done enough—having jeopardized the situation so far that the score has been set. For the most part it's been an incredibly difficult role. One that I am still not comfortable with. I have always been the fixer, the caretaker. Now I truly need the help.

Around this time, Sue Giller began to play a different role within the group. Her feelings of ambivalence about the trip were gone. She remained concerned about her weight and still doubted that she—or any of them—could make the traverse, but she was intent on reaching the Pole. She began reaching out to the others more, especially Sunniva.

But despite everyone's best efforts, the situation continued to deteriorate. On January 2, a light dusting of snow made the sleds feel much heavier. The temperature was colder at -25°C, which made a noticeable difference to them since they had less body fat than at the start of the trip.

Breathing in the cold air, Sunniva felt her bronchitis—from which she had never completely recovered—settling back into her lungs. The next day, she could only manage 3.11 miles. And the day after that was called short, too—this time after pulling 7.6 miles. At her slower pace and in the colder temperatures, Sunniva had a hard time staying warm.

Though Ann was desperate to make more miles, and Sunniva, as always, was reluctant to have the group stop on her behalf, the women all knew that it would be dangerous for Sunniva to push herself past a certain point. If she went down, if she became too ill to continue, they would all be in trouble. A rescue plane wouldn't be able to land in their current location. And it was doubtful whether the others, worn down as they were, would be able to haul her on their sleds.

DAY 56
January 3
-23/-24°C, 3.11 miles, 88°00' S, 83°24.8' W

Ann Bancroft

I try and do as many camp chores as possible to burn off steam. As I trail behind the others a short distance I suddenly break into a choppy sob. I can barely breathe. Something from deep within erupts and I register how I am feeling. Always trying to perk up—psyche up—the others leaves me a little out of touch with the depth of my feelings. With everyone tucked away in the tents, I finish putting up the antenna and walk south. Finally I turn around and look back at two small tents tucked in the sastrugi. As I tell myself the different scenarios and then try and convince myself it's not over—to stay present with this leg—I fall to my knees and weep. My mind flashes through almost five years of struggle to be here—the people who helped me—who are helping me. I push them away and take a deep breath, stop crying, and stand up.

DAY 57
January 4   -25/-24°C, 7.26 miles, 88°06.6' S, 83°28.8' W

Ann Bancroft

I really want all four of us to stand at the Pole. I thought of it all day. I also feel a need to honor this place. All the people, money, time and effort behind it.

On January 5, Day 58, the ANI staff at Patriot Hills radioed Ann some hard questions. They had to know if the women would need all their remaining food and equipment dropped off at the Pole. In other words, would there be a traverse? And if so, for how many? The team needed to make some decisions—and soon.

DAY 58
January 5   -18/-26°C, 11.7 miles, 88°16.6' S, 83°33.9' W

Anne Dal Vera

On the evening of January 5, after we made only 11.7 miles, Grant [at Patriot Hills] asked Ann to let him know the next day how many people would be coming out at the Pole. So Ann called a meeting. She said the next leg would be very hard due to the time pressure we would be under. Sue says to go on that leg you need to have a single focus on progress and let nothing else get in the way. Ann said she was concerned about my physical and emotional ability to do the rest of the traverse. Sue also said she didn't think I have what it takes emotionally. I objected and said I felt I had expressed my emotions and so it may seem that I am more emotional. Ann said she wanted to be sure I understood that my expressing my emotions was important and that isn't what concerned her. I had learned a lot about

62

expressing my emotions. What concerns her is that my physical condition affects my emotions and that affects my performance. Sue and Ann both expressed the opinion that I wouldn't get the kind of support and nurturing from either of them that I would need on such a focused and hardcore journey. I had already realized that and asked myself if I wanted to live like that for so long. I said I would think about it. Meanwhile, Ann and Sue both are concerned about Sue's weight loss and how that will affect her performance and safety down the line. In particular when they hit deep snow on the Ross Ice Shelf.

Sunniva has been hit with so many illnesses and injuries that she hasn't really been well at all. Ann said it made her very sad to think of not traveling with her further. She has been a delight to travel with. Sunniva sat with her back to me. I couldn't see her tears. She doesn't want to leave. Yet she knows "it would be irresponsible to continue."

We are committed to all four of us going to the Pole. Ann is not willing to give up the traverse. She needs our commitment that we'll push hard to the Pole to keep the dream of the traverse alive.

At the first break the next day, Anne Dal Vera told Ann that she had decided not to go on after the Pole. It was a difficult decision, one that left her feeling both sad and angry. But at least the situation was beginning to be resolved. Ann Bancroft felt some of her burden slip away. She also began to understand, a little more deeply, what this trip meant to her.

DAY 59
January 6   -20/-17°C, 11.6 miles, 88°26.7' S, 83°29.4' W

Ann Bancroft

The team—all four—getting to the Pole is the important thing to think about now. I also feel relieved by making that decision. It's what I came here to do. Not make the Pole—but to work as a team—travel as a team. Agonizing over that decision all yesterday and before was not easy. Wanted some advice from someone, but who? The traverse is still a flicker, but the four will do the Pole. I need to keep the traverse a flicker. In wrestling with all these questions, I realized that I truly came here to do the traverse. This trip has not been about being the first woman to both Poles.

Even with all the emotional turmoil, that day—Day 59—was an interesting travel day for everyone. Around noon the women were surprised to see a U.S. Air Force cargo plane coming toward them. A box dropped from the plane, and inside was a note of good wishes from the crew, plus lots of treats. Everyone's spirits lifted.

SUE GILLER
From an interview conducted by researchers at the University of Minnesota

The day after the big meeting, we're skiing along and all of a sudden Ann sees this little dot on the horizon. And pretty soon this big plane, which is a C-130, flies over us, fairly low, and we look at it and we wave and we think, "Oh, well, they're doing flights out here." And we didn't think any more about it, and it goes past us, and then about 5 minutes later apparently it turned around and went down below us, turned around and came back—I guess about two minutes later. And it was downwind, and so all of a sudden we hear this plane, and we look around and the guy's even lower. And we can see the hatch open and this little dot falls out about a quarter-mile away. So Anne Dal Vera took off her pack and her sled and skied over and got this box and skied back with it. And we opened it up, and the plane crew on their own had included a little letter in there saying, "We want to wish you the best," and signed all their names, and then inside were all these goodies, like homemade cookies and candy and lollipops,

Tootsie Roll pops and Goldfish and stuff, and then there was a rose, a fresh rose. And the first thing I noticed when we opened the package was how much we could smell that rose. It was amazing. You just hadn't smelled anything much at all until then. Just the thoughtfulness behind being in the middle of nowhere, almost to the Pole and at the end of the earth, and here comes this plane with these people who'd been following us by our radio communications and chucked out this little package. It was great. I still have the petals from that flower in my little box. I don't usually collect things, but it was just that connection with all these people who had been following us, sort of unbeknownst to us, was like, "Wow, look at this."

On that day, too, the great continent itself had a surprise in store.

DAY 59
January 6

Anne Dal Vera

In the afternoon we skied along over flat snow with some hard pack and some loose snow. Sue was in the lead, then Ann, then Sunniva, then me. I was lost in thought when I heard a long swooooosh and felt the ground shake. I stopped, my knees shaking, and looked all around me for the ghost I was sure had passed. The others were standing braced, as shocked as I was.

After a few more such episodes, we realized that the snow was settling. Sue thought the cause was a seismic field party out making recordings to see the layers of snow in the snowpack. Each of us had our own fears associated with the rumble and the movement. Ann associated it with the opening of a lead [a channel of water in ice] or the movement of a pressure ridge. Sue felt the collapse of a snow bridge across a crevasse. Sunniva knew it was an earthquake. And I looked up for an avalanche.

January 8, Day 61, was eventful as well. In the morning another U.S. Air Force plane flew over the women and tipped its wings. As always, it was odd to have their peaceful isolation broken by the jarring sound of an engine. Then, in the afternoon, the ANI Twin Otter dropped off a box of mail and some additional food, enough for them to make it to the Pole without going on shorter rations. Ann had been on the radio many nights in a row, arranging for the drop. On board that plane, they knew, were journalists who were covering Ehrling Kagge's trip. Kagge had made it to the Pole the previous day in a solo, unsupported trip from the edge of the Filchner Ice Shelf. Though there would be no journalists meeting the women at the Pole, it was exciting to think that they would be the next ones to arrive.

These events, plus the mail drop which brought news and encouragement from their friends and family at home, reminded them that their days of pulling sleds across the ice were numbered. Soon they would rejoin the world from which they came.

For the next few days, Ann found strength in the messages from her family and loved ones. She was especially moved by a note from her father, dated 12-30-92 and written on AWE stationery.

My Dear Ann,

I sense you are experiencing the loneliness of leadership at the bottom of the globe.

I steal this quote from Amundsen on Shackleton*: "No man (WOMAN) fails who sets an example of high courage, of unbroken resolution, of unshrinking endurance . . ." This now becomes Bancroft on Bancroft! In addition you add generous doses of humor and compassion. All of us associated with your journey have been enriched by you.

I love you, Dad

P.S. The check is in the mail—

---

*   Roald Amundsen and Ernest Shackleton were among the first men to explore Antarctica in the early 1900s.

In the next days Ann continued to walk the fine line between ensuring the group's overall safety and pushing for more miles so that, at least for her and Sue, the traverse might remain a possibility. She continued to monitor Sunniva closely, but was also very concerned about Anne Dal Vera, who seemed on the verge of burning out—going through periods of high energy followed by deep exhaustion and despair. Still, they all persevered. The miles and days added up. And despite pain and frustration, there was a definite thrill in approaching the South Pole.

DAY 63
January 10   -15°C, 11.5 miles, 89°14' S, 84°20' W

Sunniva Sorby

The weather is changing. It's getting colder and feels so much like the end of the world. We're on a plateau and the lighting is ever changing. It's easy to zone out. I'm getting excited. I can feel the Pole is near.

On January 12 the women spotted some tiny brown dots on the horizon. As they skied, however, the horizon line changed so much that they couldn't tell: Were the dots getting closer, farther, moving to the east or west? The next day, on a break, Sue took a GPS reading and confirmed that they were indeed looking at the South Pole base. They went to bed that night knowing that the South Pole was only 14.2 miles away—one good day of skiing.

Ann Bancroft

We skied along at a good steady pace. Sunniva and I a bit slower. I, as on many trips with length, reluctant to reach the goal. A mixture of excitement and sadness. So many years—so much focus, that I felt uncomfortable in its completion.

As we got within four miles, we were able to see movement—vehicles, etc. Bobbing lights came our way and we finally realized that it was two snowmobiles. The ice is so vast that it distorts the image. We are welcomed by three men and a woman. They are clad in overalls—sneaking away to greet us. We nibbled at the rest of our lunch and started skiing for our destination. The cold kept us going.

As we got closer, red jackets filtered out of buildings and headed our way. People yelled out various greetings of congrats and welcome. A mixed feeling upon coming to this spot. People, buildings—the smell of diesel and the sound of engines. Such the opposite of the North Pole [where there is nothing to mark the spot]. Exciting nonetheless. As we skied toward the flags [that mark the Pole], more red coats gathered there. Cameras clicking, videos moving. We tossed our video camera to someone and touched the Pole together.

We moved quickly to set up our tents and go to the gallery. It was our dinnertime. 7:30 p.m. arrival, by this time close to 9 p.m. for us. We also realized that the International Dateline made it the 15th and they were on New Zealand time. It was lunchtime for everyone at the base. We talked with people—answered questions—and soon my feet were very uncomfortable. We were still in our boots and trail clothes—moist and tired after a long day. But bread, cheese, hot drinks, and fresh faces won out and we stayed until people's work schedules won over. We eventually returned to our tents. I felt uncomfortable with the heat [of the gallery] and then the blast of cold when going outside.

Exhausted but exhilarated, Anne Dal Vera, Sunniva Sorby, Ann Bancroft, and Sue Giller touch the Pole, the first women ever to reach the South Pole on foot.

Ann was up all that night, trying to get through to her sister Carrie on the radio. She wanted to find out about the sentiment toward the trip in the United States. Was there enough interest and financial support to warrant an attempt at a traverse? But it was difficult to get through, and she felt very alone. It was her decision to make, and only hers.

The next day she pored one last time over the numbers: completing the traverse would mean doing 870 miles in just a little over thirty days. For this part of the trip Ann had planned on using a type of land sail called Upskis, which, if the wind was right, would let them cover a lot of miles quickly. But there was no way to predict how many days they would gain by using the Upskis. Recent wind patterns had not been favorable. And the short timeline allowed little room for error.

The traverse was no longer a possibility. It would be too risky. If she and Sue attempted it and failed—if they missed the ship leaving McMurdo on February 17—they would have to pay for a plane to pick them up, adding

69

roughly $350,000 to AWE's debt. Ann couldn't help but think that if they'd had a corporate sponsor, like most men's expeditions did, there would have been no question: They would have gone for it. Or, like some expeditions did, they could have simply proceeded and if necessary staged a rescue so that their insurance would pay for the plane. But as much as Ann wanted a shot at the traverse, she knew it wasn't worth compromising her integrity in that way. Furthermore, a rescue flight, especially at that time of year, was risky in itself. They could end up endangering the lives of others as well.

Finally, if she and Sue did attempt the traverse and fail, it would take away from the historic achievement the team already shared: becoming the first women to reach the South Pole on foot.

ANN BANCROFT

January 15

We will not go on. The facts are against continuing. I feel that it is the right decision but I can't stop going over the possibilities. Risk— hard to know what's responsible—a good calculated risk. No real room for failure. My heart aches. I have dreaded this moment and although it's here and passed, I feel little relief.

On the morning of January 16, the women gave a presentation to all the South Pole employees. It was then that Ann announced publicly that there would be no traverse, that the expedition was over. No one there questioned that decision. Instead there was an outpouring of understanding and respect.

SUNNIVA SORBY

January 16

There was an unusual aura of support and warmth over our decision to not continue. They understood about the time. They understood the weather and how quickly it deteriorates. Besides that we had arrived and we were safe and we were the first-ever all-women's expedition they had seen roll through there and they were proud of us!

The group stayed at the Pole for four days, waiting for the weather to clear so that the plane, ANI's Twin Otter, could take off. A small tent community sprang up: Besides the women, there were the two pilots and the Japanese science team, which arrived on January 16. On the same day, the two British explorers, Ran Fiennes and Mike Stroud, arrived at the South Pole and stayed at the camp briefly before continuing their long trek to McMurdo Base. The women visited with them in their tent. Both men had haggard, wind-burned faces, and had lost a significant amount of weight, due to the starvation research they were participating in. They looked to be in much worse shape than the women were—and yet they were going on. They could afford a rescue flight, if it became necessary.

It was hard for Ann to see them go. Not even their congratulations on being the first woman to reach both Poles did much to lessen her feelings of disappointment and longing.

ANN BANCROFT

January 16

It was quite the scene—these two groups that had become friends— one having decided to turn back, the other to go on. It took some effort on my part to stay present as it brought up my pain for our decision.

They packed up as their day was still underway. Difficult to describe the emotion in the stiff cold air—also the anguish of bidding friends goodbye to what lies ahead and their condition and my desire to travel too. My sled tempting me a quarter-mile away. I flipped my hood up as I walked along and cried. Cried hard silently, watching the two lean figures take on what I could not. The tears feel as if they've traveled from deep within.

The women were finally able to fly to Patriot Hills on January 19. But bad weather socked them in there, too—this time for about two weeks. Others were stranded as well, and the camp that was designed for about twenty-five people was overcrowded with forty. After spending so much time alone on the ice, they were uncomfortable around so many other people in such cramped quarters. Even among the four women there was some awkwardness as they all tried to adjust to being in the world again. It would take time— weeks, months, maybe even years—before they would be able to fully understand just what their journey across the ice of Antarctica had meant to them.

From Patriot Hills to Punta Arenas, from Punta Arenas to Miami, from Miami to Minnesota—finally, on February 7, the women stepped into the terminal of the Minneapolis-St. Paul International Airport. They were greeted by a cheering crowd of friends and family, AWE supporters, journalists, and more than sixty schoolchildren who had been following the expedition. It was an overwhelming, emotional scene, even more so than when they had left. Now the trip felt truly finished. The women had come full circle.

Though they didn't accomplish their original goal of completing a traverse of the continent, in many ways the women accomplished much more. In the process of becoming the first women to reach the South Pole, they had dealt head-on with adversity of all kinds. Cold. Wind. Relentless demands on their bodies. Pain, isolation, monotony, exhaustion, and despair. The difficulty of making a decision for the good of the group rather than for the good of an individual. Disappointment so deep it would never be forgotten.

They had also been blessed in many ways. They had been able to explore a part of the planet few people ever get the chance to see. They had experienced the highest level of teamwork and friendship—both on the ice and off. They knew the thrill of doing something that had never before been done. And they knew the satisfaction of inspiring others to aim high and reach out for their own goals.

SUE GILLER
From an interview conducted by researchers
at the University of Minnesota

I think, to a large extent, that being an all-women trip made the reception at the Pole more exceptional. I think because we were Americans and we were the only American group there, and we were a women's group, I think there was a tremendous amount of doubt from many people that we could do it. Certainly a lot of the people at Adventure Network [ANI] just didn't think, especially when they looked at us at only 5' 4" tall, that we could do it. But the people at the Pole have spent so much time there, they have a better feeling for the conditions, and therefore they know what we've had to travel in and what it's been like. So that makes their acknowledgment of achievement to be more powerful, because it's, in a sense, from my peers. But I do think being an all-women's group did spark everybody's interest. You know, one of the stories we like to have about this, is to try to empower all these other women to go out and do their own thing, too.

ANNE DAL VERA
From a journal entry dated January 13, 1993,
a day before reaching the South Pole:

Oh. To live passionately. That is what this has been for me.

SUNNIVA SORBY
written for the team at the Pole

While writing this I knew we would be four women standing at the Pole making history. What I did not know is how we each would be feeling at this moment. A mixed bag, no doubt.

This time is the beginning of many things to come as well as the end of 67 hard-earned trail days. From the rookie to the pro we have all managed to learn trust from each other by our actions, observations and silence. We have needed one another so much—somehow. We have learned about sharing—not just through words and things—but a common goal. One that could not be done alone. With that we did what it took to achieve this goal. Not an easy task. For some it meant putting aside our pride and fear to learn to accept help and ask for it. It meant carrying each other's weight—a word which bears a broad meaning—as I have come to accept and understand.

ANN BANCROFT

The land belongs to no one. The journey belongs to us all.

The history-making American Women's Expedition poses at the Pole.

EPILOGUE

SUMMER 2000

Even after the four team members were back in the United States, a part of the expedition remained unfinished. AWE still had a large debt, and the women were committed to paying it off. As they returned to their jobs and the normal routines of their lives, they all felt the burden of that financial obligation. They worked hard to raise money, mostly by public speaking engagements and fundraisers. It was frustrating to remain so focused on an event that had already taken place, but this was tempered with the satisfaction they felt in sharing their story with others. Several years after the expedition, the debt was paid in full.

As an organization, AWE still exists, although its name has been changed to the Ann Bancroft Foundation. Its objective is to encourage girls to pursue their dreams and tell their own stories. The foundation gives grants and holds an annual event recognizing the achievements of girls and women.

All of the team members have remained connected to Antarctica, in different ways. Ann Bancroft has a two-woman traverse planned for the 2000-2001 season. For her, the idea began even before she reached the South Pole, when she was considering whether she should attempt the traverse with Sue. The concept stayed with her. "I was waiting to see if this gnawing feeling and desire of going back would wane, and if it waned I'd just go on to something else," Ann explains. "So I was open to possibilities, but I just couldn't shake it. I had to go back. It's what I've been wanting to do since I was twelve. I was really specific then; my dream was about traversing. That is where I want to write history."

This time, Ann has taken a different approach to fundraising. She founded Base Camp Promotions, a for-profit organization made up of experienced marketing and public relations professionals. This team has taken some of the pressure off Ann, allowing her to concentrate more fully on the expedition itself.

Ann's teammate is Liv Arnesen from Oslo, Norway. In 1994 (a year after the AWE expedition), Liv became the first woman to ski solo and unsupported to the South Pole. For this trip, the women will start at Queen Maud Land and end at the Ross Ice Shelf, covering 2,400 miles. When possible, they plan on using sails to boost their mileage. There will be one resupply at the South Pole, so they won't have to put energy into arranging a drop. This means, however, that their sleds will be heavier—as much as 250 pounds.

Like Ann, Liv is a former schoolteacher, and the expedition has a strong educational component. Base Camp has teamed up with the National Center for Health Education to develop an Antarctica curriculum that will reach more than 30,000 classrooms. Base Camp is also working with the Girl Scouts to create an after-school curriculum for high school girls. This outreach to kids is a source of pride for Ann and Liv. "The teacher in me says to create something that has lasting value, something that has real credibility and viability in the classroom," Ann says.

Sunniva Sorby has returned to the Antarctic coast a dozen times, working as a history lecturer for Marine Expeditions, a cruise company based in Canada. She also continues to work for Adventure 16 in San Diego, California.

Beginning in 1995, Sunniva, too, prepared for a two-woman traverse of Antarctica. Her teammate was Uiloq Slettemark of Greenland. The women planned to depart from the edge of Berkner Island on November 1, 2000, arrive at the South Pole by January 1, 2001, and end at McMurdo Sound on the Ross Ice Shelf by mid-February. Research was to have been an important component of the trip, with scientists from Canada's Defence and Civil Institute of Environmental Medicine studying Sunniva's and Uiloq's physical and mental responses to the extreme conditions of Antarctica. The information would have been used to benefit women in the military and all women in the cold. The expedition also had an educational component in which kids from the United States, Canada, and parts of Europe would have been able to track their progress.

As with the AWE expedition, however, Sunniva's biggest challenge was raising funds. She found that many potential corporate sponsors were interested in the trip, but were slow to go the next step and actually commit money to the project. In August 2000, Sunniva and Uiloq made the difficult decision to cancel the expedition. They didn't have the financial support necessary to make the traverse. Even though the expedition never took place, the process of planning it offered a great deal of personal satisfaction. For Sunniva, the most rewarding aspects were the people she met and the opportunities she created for others during the different stages of development.

It was a coincidence that both Ann and Sunniva had planned to be on the ice at the same time. Understandably, there was a sense of competition between them, but they both emphasize that it was friendly competition. As Sunniva explains, "I one hundred percent support Ann and Liv because they're doing what I believe in. What we're all trying to do—in the big picture of young girls and women and science and research—is progressive. It will all take us one step further."

Sue Giller has been back to Antarctica twice. In 1995 she assisted a field party of geologists working for the National Science Foundation. Her job was to organize food, maintain equipment, and assess the weather and terrain for safety. She did a similar trip in 1997. Both times she was on the continent for about a month, with another month or so spent in preparation and cleanup.

These experiences—fully supported by the government, without financial pressures or the need to make miles—were very different from the AWE expedition. Still, some things were the same. In particular, she remembers the subtle variations of color within the Antarctic landscape. "The white and gray and the blue and the black. Those are the only colors you have," Sue says. "And how intricate and exquisite all of that can be in an area you would really expect to be very monotonous."

Sue continues to live in Boulder, Colorado, where she works as a computer programmer for a group of hydrological engineers. She has reached an age where she feels herself slowing down, both in drive and physical ability. She doesn't do much rock climbing anymore, but has taken up activities such as mountain biking and fishing instead. Having undertaken so many major trips, she has a lot of accomplishments to look back on. "The AWE expedition is certainly part of my identity within myself. It sort of sits back there with all the other things I've done," Sue says. "I'm proud of all of them," she adds, "but it's only part of who I am."

Anne Dal Vera has spent four summer seasons in Antarctica, supporting science research for the United States Antarctic Program. She has lived in a different location each time: the Upstream Bravo field camp, the South Pole, McMurdo, and Siple Dome. Her responsibilities have included observing the weather, loading cargo, bulldozing snow, and grooming runways. Certified as a wilderness first responder, she also provides medical support.

When the Antarctic summer is over, she returns to her job as a wilderness ranger in the Weminuche Wilderness in southwestern Colorado. "Working to preserve the enduring resource of wilderness is a way that I can give back to the world," she says.

Her memories of Antarctica, and of the team's journey to the South Pole, remain close to the surface.

"I remember the expansive feeling of pulling a sled with three companions, the only people within about 300 miles," Anne says. "The horizon stretching off in all directions, and rolling white sastrugi casting dark shadows in amazing shapes. A light blue sky with a few streaks of cirrus clouds high and thin. The sun circling around us as we skied, creating the illusion that we were skiing in circles on an endless plain. The immediate tug of the sled in the harness and my muscles developing into the sleekest form of my life. I remember the crunch of the snow under my skis and poles and the "chee-voosh" of the release of tension in the snowpack as we skied over it, breaking fragile bonds in the dry snow. I remember breathing cold, fresh air day after day, and rejoicing in the openness."

FURTHER RESOURCES

There is a documentary, *Poles Apart*, about the AWE expedition, and a website, <u>yourexpedition.com</u>, that tracks Ann Bancroft and Liv Arnesen's expedition of 2000-2001. Please note these below. They are in boldface type.

BOOKS

Alexander, Caroline. *The Endurance: Shackleton's Legendary Antarctic Expedition*. New York: Knopf, 1998.

Bylesna, Monica. *Life in the Polar Lands*. Chicago: World Book, 1997.

Cowcher, Helen. *Antarctica*. New York: Milet, 1997.

Crossley, Louise. *Explore Antarctica*. London: Cambridge University Press, 1995.

Heacox, Kim. *Antarctica: The Last Continent*. National Geographic Destinations. Washington, D.C.: National Geographic Society, 1999.

Huntford, Roland. *The Last Place on Earth: Scott and Amundsen's Race to the South Pole*. Edited by Jon Krakauer. New York: Random House, 1999.

Johnson, Rebecca. *Braving the Frozen Frontier: Women Working in Antarctica*. Minneapolis: Lerner Publishing Group, 1996. (Ages 9-12)

————. *Science on the Ice: An Antarctic Journal*. Minneapolis: Lerner Publishing Group, 1995.

Marvis, B. *The Great Polar Adventure: The Journeys of Roald Amundsen*. Illustrated by Kevin Barnes. Broomall, Pa.: Chelsea House Publishers, 1994.

Monteath, Colin. *Antarctica: Beyond the Southern Ocean*. New York: Barrons Educational Series, 1997.

Nicholson, John. *The Cruelest Place on Earth: Stories from Antarctica*. Independent Publishers Group, 1997.

Rubin, Jeff. *Lonely Planet Antarctica: A Survival Kit*. Melbourne, Australia: Lonely Planet, 1996.

Scott, Robert Falcon. *Scott's Last Expedition: The Journals*. Adapted by Beryl Bainbridge. New York: Carroll & Graf Publishers, 1996.

Soper, Tony. *Antarctica: A Guide to the Wildlife*. New York: Bradt, 1997.

Wheeler, Sara. *Terra Incognita: Travels in Antarctica*. New York: Random House, 1998.

———. *Greetings from Antarctica*. Lincolnwood, IL: NTC Publishing Group, 1999.

Worsley, Frank Arthur. *Endurance: An Epic of Polar Adventure*. New York: W.W. Norton & Co., 2000.

VIDEOS AND DVDS

Antarctica: On the Frozen Sea. Washington: National Geographic Video. VHS, 60 minutes.

Antarctica: The Last Wilderness. Washington: National Geographic Video. VHS, 60 minutes.

Ernest Shackleton and the Endurance Expedition. 1919. Distributed by Milestone Film & Video, Harrington Park, NJ. Tinted and toned by the British Film Institute's National Film and Television Archive. VHS, DVD, 88 minutes.

Ernest Shackleton: To the End of the Earth. West Long Branch, NJ: Kultur Video, 1999. Great Adventurers Series. VHS, 50 minutes, color.

Heart of Antarctica: Journey to the Ice. Volume 1. Venice, CA: TMW Media Group, 1998. VHS, 20 minutes, color, study guides.

Heart of Antarctica: The End of the Earth and Beyond. Volume 2. Venice, CA: TMW Media Group, 1998. VHS, 20 minutes, color, study guides.

90 Degrees South: With Scott to the Antarctic. 1933. Distributed by Milestone Film & Video, Harrington Park, NJ. VHS, DVD, Laserdisc, 72 minutes, black & white.

Poles Apart. Minneapolis: Lead Dog Productions, 2000. VHS, 86 minutes, color. A documentary about the AWE expedition and the 1992-93 traverse by Mike Stroud and Sir Ranulph Fiennes.

Robert Falcon Scott. West Long Branch, NJ: Kultur Video, 1999. Great Adventurers Series. VHS, 50 minutes, color.

Shackleton: Escape from Antarctica. West Long Branch, NJ: Kultur Video, 1999. VHS, 52 minutes, color.

With Byrd at the South Pole. 1930. Distributed by Milestone Film & Video, Harrington Park, NJ. VHS, DVD, Laserdisc, 82 minutes, black & white.

WEB SITES

Alfred Wegener Institute
http://www.awi-bremerhaven.de/ClickLearn/index.html

Amundsen-Scott South Pole Station
http://www.spole.gov/

Ann Bancroft and Liv Arnesen's traverse 2000 site
http://www.yourexpedition.com

Antarctic Connection
http://www.antarcticconnection.com/

Australian Antarctic Program
http://www.antdiv.gov.au/

Glacier: Antarctica's Journey through Time and Space
www.glacier.rice.edu/land/5_antarcticicesheetjourney.html

Live from Antarctica 2
www.passporttoknowledge.com/antarctica2/main/o_index.html

National Science Foundation (Office of Polar Programs)
http://www.nsf.gov/od/opp/

Scientific Committee on Antarctic Research
http://www.scar.org./

70 South
http://www.70south.com/home

Teachers Experiencing Antarctica
http://tea.rice.edu/tea_aboutus.html

INDEX

DATE DUE